TURNING POINTS

Let the
Crow's Feet
& Laugh Lines
Come!

© 2010 by Barbour Publishing, Inc.

ISBN 978-1-60260-451-3

All rights reserved. No part of this publication may be reproduced or transmitted for commercial purposes, except for brief quotations in printed reviews, without written permission of the publisher.

Churches and other noncommercial interests may reproduce portions of this book without the express written permission of Barbour Publishing, provided that the text does not exceed 500 words or 5 percent of the entire book, whichever is less, and that the text is not material quoted from another publisher. When reproducing text from this book, include the following credit line: "From *Let the Crow's Feet and Laugh Lines Come!*, published by Barbour Publishing, Inc. Used by permission."

Scripture quotations marked KJV are taken from the King James Version of the Bible.

Scripture quotations marked NIV are taken from the HOLY BIBLE, NEW INTERNATIONAL VERSION®. NIV®. Copyright © 1973, 1978, 1984 by International Bible Society. Used by permission of Zondervan. All rights reserved.

Scripture quotations marked NASB are taken from the New American Standard Bible, © 1960, 1962, 1963, 1968, 1971, 1972, 1973, 1975, 1977, 1995 by The Lockman Foundation. Used by permission.

Scripture quotations marked NKJV are taken from the New King James Version®. Copyright © 1982 by Thomas Nelson, Inc. Used by permission. All rights reserved.

Scripture quotations marked MSG are from *THE MESSAGE*. Copyright © by Eugene H. Peterson 1993, 1994, 1995, 1996, 2000, 2001, 2002. Used by permission of NavPress Publishing Group.

Scripture quotations marked NLT are taken from the *Holy Bible*, New Living Translation, copyright © 1996, 2004. Used by permission of Tyndale House Publishers, Inc. Wheaton, Illinois 60189, U.S.A. All rights reserved.

Scripture quotations marked CEV are from the Contemporary English Version, Copyright © 1991, 1992, 1995 by American Bible Society. Used by permission.

Scripture quotations marked NCV are taken from the New Century Version of the Bible, copyright © 2005 by Thomas Nelson, Inc. Used by permission.

Scripture quotations marked NLV are taken from the Holy Bible, New Life Version, Copyright 1969, 1976, 1978, 1983, 1986, Christian Literature International, P.O. Box 777, Canby, OR 97013. Used by permission.

Published in association with the Books & Such Literary Agency, 52 Mission Circle, Suite 122, PMB 170, Santa Rosa, CA 95409-5370, www.booksandsuch.biz

Published by Barbour Publishing, Inc., P.O. Box 719, Uhrichsville, Ohio 44683, www.barbourbooks.com

Our mission is to publish and distribute inspirational products offering exceptional value and biblical encouragement to the masses.

Member of the Evangelical Christian Publishers Association

Printed in the United States of America.

TURNING POINTS

Dena Dyer

Let the Crow's Feet & Laugh Lines Come!

Rediscovering Beauty
and Self-Worth at Any Age

BARBOUR
PUBLISHING

Dedication

For Jordan and Jackson

Contents

Overview.. 7

Introduction... 9

Chapter 1:
   Ask Yourself the Hard Questions 11

Chapter 2:
   Accept Your Changing Body..................... 35

Chapter 3:
   Make the Most of What You've Got.............. 57

Chapter 4:
   Love Out Loud................................. 79

Chapter 5:
   Keep the Faith................................ 105

Chapter 6:
   Cultivate Community........................... 131

Chapter 7:
   Invest in What Matters........................ 155

Chapter 8:
   Become Audacious.............................. 179

Chapter 9:
   Giggle, Dance, and Sing 199

Overview

Since our theme is the "sea of changes" we're going through as aging women, each chapter will be divided into sections:

- *The Drift*—an introduction to the issues covered in the chapter
- *Ballast*—the biblical aspects we should consider as we deal with those specific issues
- *Setting a Course*—suggestions in facing the issues, taken from the Bible and the formative life experiences of other maturing women
- *Smooth Sailing*—a chapter wrap-up that provides important "takeaway" points from the chapter, as well as empowering Bible verses for you to meditate on and perhaps memorize

Do you feel that you're in uncharted water? You're not alone! God is our compass, our guide, and our goal. And many women have sailed before you, facing the challenges you're experiencing, with beauty and grace. Together, with God's help, we can reach our destination with our sanity, spirit, and sense of humor intact!

Introduction

You know those books on getting older that list all the blessings aging brings, while glossing over the hard stuff?

This is not one of those books.

Instead, in this volume, we're going to get real and honest. We'll discuss all the hard parts of aging—adapting to the "sea of changes" in your body and relationships, losing loved ones, saying good-bye to old dreams, and saying hello to new ones. We'll also touch on the lighter issues, such as having aches and pains in parts you didn't realize you had, losing things you wish you didn't need, and finding hairs in places previously bare. And, yes, we'll also talk about the good parts of getting older, discovering together how we can meet the challenges inherent in aging, with grace and humor.

In the following nine chapters, we'll cover several areas in which we need to give God full access, and we'll listen in as godly, glowing, and gracious women reveal how they've seen God move in their lives.

As we do, we'll raise the curtain on many of the issues facing us as the calendar pages drop. Together, we'll find out what God has to say about them so that we can experience His presence, peace, and hope in the midst of our aging process. If we want God to be glorified in us as we age, let's strive to discover the difference between just getting older and getting better.

Chapter 1

Ask Yourself the Hard Questions

*Youth is not a time of life, it's a state of mind.
You are as young as your faith, as old as your doubt;
as young as your self-confidence, as old as your fear;
as young as your hope, as old as your despair.*
UNKNOWN

THE DRIFT

Aging used to be revered, not feared. For centuries, several generations lived together, and grandparents were an integral part of a child's existence. Elderly people's hard-earned wisdom helped younger people cope with daily life. But sometime in the twentieth century, as travel became cheaper, families began to spread out. Nursing homes popped up to help care for frail bodies, and the media spread the lie that "younger is better."

Now, we fear the natural process God created in our bodies. We dread slowing down, getting sick, and putting on weight. We have believed the lie that we will become useless if we can't do the same things we've done before. We're terrified of losing our faculties, our finances, and our families. And each passing year, the changes we experience physically seem to back up the notion that getting older is a crime, or at least a shame.

Here are just a few things we may begin learning as we get older:

- Our energy seems to lag at the very moment we need it.
- Our health is more precarious than we once thought, and much more precious than we once knew.
- We've experienced more of life's ups and downs than we could have imagined in our twenties, but we still

don't know all the answers.
- Just when we start to think we're getting ahead in financial matters, life goes and throws us a huge curve.

But there are also many wonderful things that happen to us as the clock ticks. We may not have the get-up-and-go we once had, but we gain the perspective and maturity that make life so much richer!

- If married, we're finding that a "mature" marriage doesn't get easier—but it does get sweeter.
- Our kids and our parents, if we have them, are giving us lots of gray hair. . .and tons of laughs.
- Friendships that we thought would last have faded, but then God has also surprised us with new, better friends—of all ages.
- Every day there's a new reason to fear—but also a new reason to rejoice.
- God is faithful. His promises are real. And He is with us all the time.

Can you relate? Although you've already learned quite a bit, are you also asking yourself a lot of questions—more each day, in fact—as the years tick by? Questions such as:

- When did my wild oats turn into shredded wheat?

- How fast is my body going to go downhill? And is there any way to slow the process?
- Why do I feel like I'm my parents' parent all of a sudden?
- Will my kids or close relatives put me in a nice nursing home?
- Will I ever get to retire? Travel? Find the perfect mate? Have grandkids?
- Can I blame global warming for my hot flashes?

See if you recognize your own issues as other women share some of their biggest concerns.

Mindy, a widowed mom of two grown kids, wonders if she'll remarry, and if so, will her children like her new husband?

Beth admits, "Every morning it seems like something else hurts or doesn't work properly. And my memory is slipping."

Kathi wonders if she'll have enough energy and strength to do all the things God has called her to do.

Selina is single and worries about losing her employment—especially since she has specialized job training in a single field—and insurance.

Leah is divorced and has never had kids. She worries about ending up all alone.

Diane asks, "Will my finances last throughout my lifetime?"

Lane doesn't want to look old. "I don't mind wrinkles," she says, "I just don't want very many!"

Joanne says, "Well, besides worrying about brain tumors, heart disease, Alzheimer's, blood clots, osteoporosis, and incontinence, my biggest concern would have to be the fear that my hairdresser won't be able to cover all of my gray hair. That and my recurring dream where all of my teeth fall out."

Marcia doesn't want to become a burden to her children.

Bonnie says, "I want to keep active and yet my body puts limitations on me. . . . I want to still be a good wife even with the changes in my body. . . . I want to be actively involved as a mentor to my adult children and my precious grandchildren. . . . I want to be a loving and supportive daughter with my aging parents even though I'm stretched very thin already. . . . I want to nourish and savor the times I share with good friends, and last but not least, I want to continue to grow spiritually and stretch my mind so that I can continue to be a wife, mother, grandmother, daughter, sister, and friend who can stay involved and contribute to the lives of those I love and care about."

And Trish says, "I worry about rearranging my life so much for my children that once they are gone or no longer need me, I won't know what to do. I worry about my children. Will they live out their faith in Christ? Will they wander? Make bad choices? And I worry about our parents—will we be able to care for them as they grow older? What health problems will they run into? How will we balance caring for our kiddos and our parents during the sandwich-generation years? Basically, I worry a lot."

Let's face it. As we get older, life throws more curveballs at us, and we can easily get overwhelmed. Or God takes too long in answering our prayers, and we think He's forgotten us. But if we let Him journey with us, He promises to give us peace, courage, and His perspective. He also gives us choices, which can lead us to a dead end or the place of victory we're destined for. He longs to become our one constant when life's huge waves rock our boat.

BALLAST

God is constant.

All of us have been disappointed and betrayed. Sometimes, we've been shocked by the actions of fellow believers. And at other times, a friend or family member inflicts hurt so deep we wonder if we'll ever trust again. It can make us hesitant to trust God. We wonder, will He let us down, too?

A character in *The Count of Monte Cristo* was convinced God—if He even existed—had forgotten him. In the film, which is based on the book by Alexander Dumas, Edmond Dantes is framed for treason by his best friend. He's then locked away in a remote prison for thirteen years, while his family and fiancée are told he's been executed. While in prison, Edmond meets a fellow inmate, a priest.

As the man of God mentors Edmond, he encourages the lad to forgive his friend, forget plans of revenge, and acknowledge that God is real. But Edmond will have none of it. You see, Edmond gave up on God long before he met the priest, during his first few agonizing years in prison. Before the priest suddenly dies, he urges Edmond to forget vengeance and remember God has a plan for his life. Edmond tells the priest, "I don't believe in God." And the priest says, "It doesn't matter. He believes in you."

That scene is powerful, because it reminds the viewer that emotions don't affect God's reality. His love never changes, and His presence never leaves us.

Friends may desert us. . .but God won't.

Our bodies will fail us. . .but God won't.

Children may leave us. . .but God won't.

Parents will die. . .but God won't.

Bank accounts may falter. . .but God won't.

Family members will disappoint us. . .but God won't.

Our dreams may crumble. . .but God won't.

Dear readers, if we will hold on to the truth that God is perfect in love, constant in grace, and holy in purpose, it can comfort us as we experience the ticking of the clock and the sometimes-frightening changes in our bodies, relationships, and world.

God is our peace.

As in every issue of our lives, we must look to God and His answers in order to find peace. He holds the key to all our questions. And through the power of the Holy Spirit, He led ordinary men to pen the only true answer book in the world—God's Word.

Let's turn to the Bible and look at the story of Hannah, which demonstrates God is our peace in an ever-changing world.

> *The young woman took a deep breath. The bread in front of her looked like stone.*
>
> *"Hannah, you haven't eaten in days," her husband Elkanah said gently. "You need nourishment."*
>
> *Elkanah's other wife shot Hannah a menacing look. "Maybe that's why she's barren. She's too skinny."*
>
> *"Hush, Pen," Elk said. "Leave her alone."*
>
> *Peninnah glared at Hannah. "Sure, I'll leave her alone. Just like the Lord has."*
>
> *Hannah stifled a sob and pushed away from the table. She ran out the door and into the place of worship, falling on her knees at the altar.*
>
> *"Oh, Lord God," she cried. "You know I'm Your servant, but I am so miserable! Please, let me have a son. If You do, I will give him to You for as long as he lives!"*
> (author's paraphrase)

All of us who have experienced the pain of waiting for answers can relate to Hannah. The Bible says she prayed so fervently that the priest thought she was drunk. Nevertheless, she felt better after having poured her heart out to the Lord.

Hannah didn't yet have an answer to her request (the happy ending comes later in the book—1 Samuel 1:19–2:11), but she knew the Lord well enough to leave her problems at His altar. She refused to worry herself sick, and she didn't take revenge on her rival. Unlike Edmond Dantes in *The Count of Monte Cristo*, she knew God could be trusted, that He had her best interests at heart, and that He would deal out justice to her enemies—in His own way and time.

How many times have we given our problems—financial crises, health issues, fears and doubts about aging—to the Lord and then taken them back, convinced we could work them out on our own if we just knew more or tried harder?

Often, we *say* we believe in God's goodness, but then we turn around and act as if it's all up to us. We need to be more like Hannah—fervent in prayer and childlike in trust. How much simpler our lives would be if we followed her example! Remember, "God is love, and. . .as we live in God, our love grows more perfect. . . . Such love has no fear, because perfect love expels all fear" (1 John 4:16–18 NLT). And having fear expelled, we have peace.

God gives us courage.
What do you fear as you get older?

- Are you afraid to receive a certain diagnosis?
- If you're married, do you wonder if your relationship will survive all the changes you're both going through?
- Do you dread looking in the mirror?
- Does the thought of becoming dependent on someone cause you anxiety?
- Do you wrestle with God at night over financial matters?
- If you have kids, are you having panic attacks when you think about your children's choices?

Whatever your concerns, take them to God. He can be trusted and will give you courage to face anything and everything.

Sally needed courage when she had to face a fractured and splintering marriage after twenty-seven years of being wed to her best friend. She says, "Everybody has at least one dark closet in their life, stuffed full of things they no longer use, but can't bring themselves to throw away. My marriage felt like that closet, crowded with emotions hastily crammed into dark corners, a bulging door shut tight. Hairline fractures in the walls surrounding the door frame threatened the entire structure of our relationship. The last thing my husband

and I tried to stuff into our closet was another disagreement over money. That's when I realized we needed the help of a professional counselor."

In the beginning, Sally and her husband both attended the weekly therapy sessions, but after a few months, her husband was too uncomfortable to continue—and she was too desperate to stop.

One day, after a particularly draining session, Sally knelt beside her bed and cried. "Be with me, Lord, please! If You are not with me, I can't survive this."

As her pleadings wore on, she found herself lying on the floor, flat on her face, head in her arms, begging ever more earnestly, until she heard a thought in her mind that was not her own.

"Instead of Me being with you, why don't you be with Me?"

Then, Sally suddenly remembered a scripture passage from Luke 15:11–32, the story of the prodigal son. She recalls, "As if God had switched a light on in my gloomy closet, I realized the servants in the story did not strain their eyes, searching the road for the wayward child—they simply watched their master and waited for his word. They would know the instant the wandering offspring turned his foot to return home, because they would see it on their master's face and hear the cry of joy in his voice. I knew then that waiting with Him was where God wanted me to be."

And in that moment, Sally says she could see her

emotions in the perspective of what they really were, not what she had imagined them to be. As she sifted each memory, she watched her Master's face and knew what she should discard and what she should keep.

Therapy continued for months, but she could feel real healing begin during that counseling session with the Wonderful Counselor, the Prince of Peace—Jesus.

Sally's experience is evidence of one of the most amazing and fulfilling aspects about maturing. As we get older, our relationship to God changes. Sometimes those changes are frightening, but they're always for our good. After years of prayers, we begin to see the pattern of His answers. From the hindsight of aging, we see God's purposes more fully and start to trust Him more.

In return, He gives us more of Himself. . .and it's awesome! And our burgeoning trust in Him gives us the courage to face anything!

God gives us His perspective.

Another wonderful aspect of getting older—although this one depends on whether or not we'll *let* God change us—is that we begin to care more about the things that are truly important and less about some of the superficial things that used to bother us the most.

Amy is an example to us in this regard. Last year she decided to ditch the traditional resolutions, such as lose weight, get in shape, or read the entire Bible in a year. She said, "Those are good things, but I've found that this only leads to guilt when I fall short of keeping those best-intention promises to myself. Instead, I decided to choose a life theme for the entire year."

Amy's theme this year is "whatever." Getting older has given her some newfound freedoms. She's learning to let go of who she'd thought she'd be by this point in her life, and instead embrace who she is. Amy's trying to spend less time worrying about what others think of her and more time thinking of others.

Amy says too many of her years have been wasted on trying to be something she's not and trying to please those she can't.

So whenever someone acts ugly toward her, she's saying, "Whatever." When she says something stupid or is misunderstood, she thinks, *Whatever*. If she puts herself out there, makes an extra effort but gets little to nothing in response, Amy's attitude is "whatever." (And this "whatever" isn't sarcastic—it's freeing. It's a letting go, a release of expectations. This "whatever" is a shrug of the shoulders with a chuckle in the throat.)

Says Amy: "Life is too short, and I have too much to be grateful for to agonize over the trivial. This isn't an attempt to be callous, cruel, or clueless. This is a means of not only survival but joyous living. I can free up others to say, 'Whatever' right back at me. I can let go of the endless soul searching for what is wrong with me and appreciate what is flawed, broken, and redeemable. I give myself a break and, in turn, give you one."

Amy's choosing to focus on one of my all-time favorite scriptures: "Whatever is true, whatever is noble, whatever is right, whatever is pure, whatever is lovely, whatever is admirable—if anything is excellent or praiseworthy—think about such things. . . . And the God of peace will be with you" (Philippians 4:8–9 NIV).

I love Amy's attitude! Like her, I've chosen a life theme for the past three years, and it's been a delightful journey to see how God has affirmed those words in my life. Each fall, I pray about the next year's theme, and try to listen to what God is impressing upon me. One year, the theme was "refuge"—and we moved to a new town a few months after God revealed that word to me. How timely!

Why not choose a life theme for yourself? Then, as the next few months unfold, you can look up scriptures that mention your "theme" word—and stay open to things God will illuminate to you as you meditate on the theme.

If you take this challenge, you won't be disappointed. God's surprises are exquisite. . .and as constant as His word, His presence, and His goodness—if we have eyes to see. He longs to be in a daily conversation with us, and our concerns are ultra important to Him, because He's our Father, and we are His precious daughters.

God gives us choices.

Besides God's unfailing peace, courage, and perspective, He gives us free will, a choice about how to live our lives. The women we have watched grow older can give us comfort, as well as challenge us, as we mature.

Nanaw (my mom's mom) died nine years ago. She was one of my best friends, whose door was always open to me. Nanaw was an artist and writer, as well as an art teacher. She learned to use the computer in her eighth decade and wrote two books when she was in her eighties. At times, she and my grandfather would dance to the background music in the grocery store, much to my mother's chagrin. While they waltzed around the frozen food, my mother hid behind the stacks of canned goods, praying no one would see her. Their defense? "We can't let this good music go to waste!" Nanaw inspired me to live life to the fullest, and not be afraid to try new things. She helped me and others around her to let go of their worries and embrace life.

Nanaw lived her life with abandon, in every sense of the word. She went to a Baylor University basketball game with her boyfriend the night before she died of a heart attack. It was devastating to lose her so suddenly, but I'm very thankful she never suffered. In fact, she'd prayed to die suddenly, because being dependent on someone or being debilitated would have crushed her. For her sake, I'm glad her death happened the way it did.

My other grandmother, Nana, died as I was writing this chapter. For the past several years, she had been in a nursing home, and it pained me to see her there—because she had no quality of life. The nurses all loved her, though, and instead of becoming a bitter woman, she became sweeter with age.

Nana's life was hard, and she made the best of it. She was a loving, loyal, thoughtful mother and grandmother, who always shared what she had, though sometimes it wasn't much, with her family. She was supportive of her kids' dreams and proud of all her grandchildren.

But one thing she didn't do as she got older was focus on her health. She and her late husband, Ted, our step-grandfather, rarely ventured beyond the four walls of their home, and they loved to eat fried foods, soda, and ice cream—things that may have contributed to the mental and physical decline she experienced over the past few years. Before Ted died of a heart attack a few years ago, he sat with her every day, all day, in the nursing home. That loyalty was—and is—inspiring.

When we look at the maturing women (and men) around us, we should ask ourselves, who do we want to emulate? What do we want our older years to look like? God has given us free will, and we can make certain choices that add up over time. Do we want to cultivate a generous spirit? To display loyalty to our spouses or other loved ones through thick and thin? Do we desire to be creative and free-spirited? To cheer our family members on and rejoice in their successes? To stay active well into our eighties or nineties? To continue learning new things? To live life with abandon?

SETTING A COURSE

Of course, we can't control everything—or even most things—about getting older. But we do have *some* control. We can age badly or well, and much of that depends on our attitude, relationship to the Lord and others, and how we take care of our bodies (more on that in a later chapter). The small daily decisions we make add up to a lifetime of behavior, some good and some bad. And those choices affect our quality of life and the legacy we leave behind.

Ask yourself these questions:

- When you're gone, what do you want to be known for? As a kind person, a generous philanthropist, a good teacher, a fun grandma?
- What are your goals? To finish a degree, retire early, minister to more people, etc.?
- What does God say about your goals and dreams? Do they line up with scripture, or do you need to pray and ask God to change your heart?

- Are you following God every day? Do you ask God to live through you daily? Do you take time to sit at the Lord's feet to hear His plans and thoughts toward you? Do you read scripture? Pray? Fellowship with other believers? Serve others with gratitude and a pure heart?
- Are you listening to the world's opinion about getting older, or do you listen to God's viewpoint? The Bible praises aging and the wisdom acquired with age. It rarely comments on people's specific physical qualities, and instead focuses on their inner beauty and graciousness of spirit—or lack of it!
- Who do you want to "look like"? Who are your heroes? What have they done that you can emulate? What things do you not want to copy?
- Are you overwhelmed with the thought of getting older? If so, why? Maybe you're concentrating on all the hardships and none of the joys inherent in maturing. Are you letting Satan lie to you? If so, begin to pinpoint those things he's whispering to you, and ask God for help in replacing the lies with His truth.

Jesus is the ultimate hero—that goes without saying. But who else do you want to emulate? And why do you long to be like them? Some of our earthly heroines can be grandmothers, girlfriends, mothers, writers, singers, or mentors/teachers.

Of course, we want to be the best version of "us" that we

can be. But there are so many things we can learn by taking note of how other women age gracefully. Think about your role models, and why you admire them.

Martha Bolton, a humor author who's written for Bob Hope, says, "My hero is Mary Tyler Moore. We're both longtime diabetics, and she has successfully juggled career, family, and the daily challenges of health issues. And on top of that, she's made it through menopause! My other heroes are my aunts Clara, Sibyl, and Martha. These stylish women are all almost, or in their nineties, and are still going strong, with their sense of humor and sense of purpose intact. One drives a bright red car, and another still mows her own lawn!"

Carol's aunt Helen is her role model: "She has always been the most cheerful person with a positive outlook on everything. She knows the importance of taking care of herself. Helen's had her share of health issues, but she never complains. She has outlived three husbands, two of which died much too young. She lost a son when he was just in his twenties. And Helen's daughter went in for a routine surgery and died of complications. Traumatized over the death of his mother, one of her grandsons committed suicide the next day."

Carol notes, "Obviously, Helen has had much more than her fair share of burdens. But, her faith in Jesus Christ has gotten her through the sad times. She continues to smile. We just had a family reunion this past weekend. Helen's son drove her to the reunion from six hours away. She wouldn't miss it for anything! So, at age eighty-two, sitting in a wheelchair, there was Helen, smiling as always! As everyone else complained about the extreme Texas heat, Helen just sat there smiling and being thankful for so much. We could all learn from her example."

These women can teach us much about aging well. Whatever our goals, we can partner with God and surrender as He continues to mold and, yes, even use us, well into our senior years. Let's pray that as we get older, God will give us the desire to be the women God has called us to be.

It won't be easy. We must listen daily to what He's asking of us, and obey. We must also trust that God's plans are "to prosper you and not to harm you. . .to give you hope and a future" (Jeremiah 29:11 NIV). We have to ask ourselves hard questions, and let God and others ask us some difficult questions as well. Oh yes, one more thing: We must be willing to deal with the things He reveals to us—some of them difficult—along the way.

SMOOTH SAILING

Now that you've read this chapter and asked yourself some of the hard questions, remember that God's Word always holds the answers to life's issues. In an uncertain world, God is our surety. He is our "lifeboat" in what can sometimes be very deep waters. When we need an anchor, He holds us. When we're uncertain, He gives us peace. When we're scared, He gives us courage. And when we need a new perspective, He gives us a new vision. Finally, He gives us choices, allowing us to steer the boat of our lives toward the goals we have. Whatever our needs, He will provide them. Whatever our questions, He is the answer.

Try writing the following verses on index cards and taking them with you wherever you go. Meditate upon them or, better yet, memorize them so they will be written upon your heart.

- *"The LORD himself goes before you and will be with you; he will never leave you nor forsake you. Do not be afraid; do not be discouraged."*
  DEUTERONOMY 31:8 NIV

- *You will keep in perfect peace him whose mind is steadfast, because he trusts in you. Trust in the LORD forever, for the LORD, the LORD, is the Rock eternal.*
  ISAIAH 26:3–4 NIV

- *"Blessed is she who believed, for there will be a fulfillment of those things which were told her from the Lord."*
  LUKE 1:45 NKJV

- *Let us run with endurance the race that is set before us, looking unto Jesus, the author and finisher of our faith.*
  HEBREWS 12:1–2 NKJV

- *"Be strong and courageous. Do not be afraid or terrified because of them, for the LORD your God goes with you; he will never leave you nor forsake you."*
  DEUTERONOMY 31:6 NIV

- *And the work of righteousness will be peace, and the service of righteousness, quietness and confidence forever.*
  ISAIAH 32:17 NASB

Chapter 2

ACCEPT YOUR CHANGING BODY

*You know you're getting old when everything hurts.
And what doesn't hurt doesn't work.*
HY GARDNER

◐ THE DRIFT

Have you seen the T-shirt that says, "I'm so far over the hill, I've started up the next one?" Sometimes our bodies seem determined to betray us as we age.

The other day, our workplace had a cookout/swim party. So I had to get into my suit for the first time in a year, and it was not a pretty sight. Since (like many women) I'm getting thicker as I get older, my suit is a "smart" suit, which means it's made of forgiving fabric and is black with vertical—not horizontal—stripes, for obvious reasons.

Unfortunately, the help my "smart" suit gives me stops with the tummy panel and leaves my glaringly pale arms and thighs fully exposed. As I stuffed my pasty, postpubescent body into the spandex sausage-casing, I rethought my fitness regime. By the time I got one leg through its hole, I was vowing to do one hundred leg lifts a day. After hoisting my other leg up and through, I decided to perform several hundred sit-ups before breakfast. And after sucking in, pulling the swimsuit over my belly, and sticking my arms through, I decided *that* was workout enough.

Swimsuit season makes many women reconsider their "absolutely not, never, no way" stance on plastic surgery. The reality of sagging and puckered skin, pooching tummies, and varicose veins leads many women to lose their common sense. Liposuction starts to look attractive instead of dangerous. And the cost of tummy tucks seems doable—if you just raid the retirement fund.

But if we can stop beating up ourselves long enough to consider the costs, not to mention the risks, of plastic surgery, we may just return to our senses. The only reason most of us would even consider it? Our culture places a high value on outer appearances, and we tend to get swept up in all the midriff-baring mania.

You've seen them, the so-called reality shows where real women get transformed—via plastic surgery, dental work, exercise, wardrobe changes, hair extensions, and extreme diets—into supermodels. You may have even wished that you could be selected as a participant. I know I've been tempted once or twice to *at least* get my teeth whitened again or *at most* pay for one of those really expensive, really restrictive diet plans.

But if you look closely, you might discover that the ladies on those shows (not so much the men, who retain some semblance of their former selves) all come out looking alike. Creepily Stepfordian.

Instead of feeling inspired, we should instead be repulsed at the way the current culture (especially the popular media) makes women, especially aging ones, loathe our bodies. No news flash here: We are an appearance-driven, celebrity-obsessed, beauty-addicted society.

Do you realize how ridiculous it is that we expect ourselves, and even other women, to never look older? We think we can keep our faces and figures from our teenage or college years just by trying hard enough. It's ludicrous—and a lie.

We see models or actresses who never seem to mature, and wonder, "Why can't I do that?" Well, it's because they *have* to look good—or they'll lose their jobs. So they pay for expensive operations, put themselves through painful weekly (or even daily) procedures, and go into seclusion each time their bodies rebel. And then if they're unlucky—or human—enough to have even a smidgen of a bad hair day, the stalkerazzi swarm all over them and sell their "ugly" pictures to the highest bidder.

How would you like that pressure, besides dealing with all the normal physical changes (hot flashes, sleep disturbances, mood swings) aging brings? Those gals spend literally hours a day at the gym (*not* with their friends or family members) so that they can continue their careers.

Author Lane Jordan has noticed this pressure to be perfect. She says, "With many more magazines on the market and the explosion of television channels, women are now bombarded daily with seeing other women who are so much more beautiful in face and body than they ever could be. And how tragic this is! If we could see into the heart of so many of these 'stars,' we might see lives that are empty and hollow."

So what's the answer? Lane says, "Nothing is more important to a person's self-esteem and value than discovering how God views us. When we shift our focus from the world's point of view of what's beautiful and turn instead to what God says, we will realize that each one of us—wrinkles, arthritis and all—is *so* beautiful to Him! God sent His Son and His precious Holy Spirit to us to show how much He loves, cherishes, and values us. My prayer is that women would stop each day and thank God for all the blessings they have and not focus on how their body is decaying. For as our bodies fade away, our Spirit is being renewed for Christ!"

Bottom line: We are a sad, sick, self-absorbed society. Even Christians have fallen for the lie that "your value is determined by what you look like." Ladies, we must determine to listen to the Lord, and not the world. We are so beautiful to God. So is every person on this planet. We are made in God's image—and we are loved by our heavenly Father as His glorious children. The scriptures teach us that when God looks at us, He sees us through the filter of Jesus—the lens of grace.

FamilyNet television personality and radio host Lorri Allen has dealt with increasing media pressure as she's gotten older. For many years, producers have told her that she wasn't thin enough or pretty enough to work in her dream field of television broadcasting. But she chose to listen to God, and not the world. She believed God had called her to spread His love and message through that medium, and she never gave up. She's beautiful and charming, by the way—and I

Accept Your Changing Body

can't imagine anyone telling her she needed to improve to be on TV. But that's the way that the media system operates, evidently.

She notes, "Wrinkles will win, our vitality will fade, and those platitudes moms everywhere are famous for saying will come true: Pretty is as pretty does, you can't judge a book by its cover, and if you're pretty on the inside, you'll be pretty on the outside." Lorri says that you become pretty on the inside by "counting your blessings, instead of dwelling on your curses.

Determine to love others. Decide once and for all that God does take care of you. Those three steps will give you a beautiful smile, inspire sparkling eyes of compassion, and erase the worry lines."[1]

---

[1] From the essay, "Face Value" by Lorri Allen. 2008. Used with author's permission. For more information, see www.Lorri.com.

◐ BALLAST

Speaking of inner beauty, you've probably heard the story of Esther. She was a Jew, living pretty much in obscurity until King Xerxes got mad at his wife Vashti and decided to replace her. Xerxes didn't want just any queen—so his men rounded up all the virgins in his kingdom and put them through beauty treatments for a solid year. By the time they were done, the women probably felt like a million bucks and looked like *Deal or No Deal*'s suitcase-holders—perfectly coiffed, perfumed, and shiny.

But out of all the beauties, Esther stood out. She became Xerxes' favorite, and he doted on her. However, the king's right-hand man, Haman, hated Esther's cousin Mordecai who had raised her as his own after her parents died. Mordecai refused to grovel at Haman's feet, so Haman got the king to agree to annihilate the Jews.

When Mordecai learned about the plot, he asked Esther to plead with Xerxes to spare the Jews. She hesitated, for anyone who approached the emotionally unstable king without being invited could be putting his or her neck on the chopping block. At this point, Mordecai did some plain talking to his niece.

"Listen, girl," he said, "don't think that you won't die in the Jew-killings just because you're a favorite of the king." And then he uttered one of the most-loved passages in the

Bible: "Who knows? Perhaps you have come to royal dignity for such a time as this" (Esther 4:14, author's paraphrase).

Esther's response was immediate, as if she realized she had gotten just the kick in the pants she needed. Esther asked Mordecai to have the Jews fast and pray for her, and then she went before the king in one of the Bible's most fearless acts. God used her bravery to save His children, and the king, impressed with her courage even more than her beauty, called off his plans.

Though God is not specifically mentioned in the book of Esther, He is behind the scenes, and Mordecai even suggested that he was confident help would come for God's chosen people—with or without Esther's help.

We can glean a lot from Esther's story: She probably stood out from the other pageant princesses vying for Vashti's crown not because she had the best hair, but because she loved God with all her heart. And when her back was against the wall, her true inner beauty shone through. Instead of cowering in a corner, Esther came out swinging (with God's help), and her boldness and faith endeared her even more to the king. We're believers in Jesus Christ in a world that is increasingly hostile to Him. When we become more like Him, and listen to His truth instead of Satan's lies, our inner loveliness will shine the light of His love into the darkness around us. And when we allow Him to make us bold and brave, we'll endear ourselves even more to our heavenly King.

Ephesians 2:10 says, "For we are God's workmanship, created in Christ Jesus to do good works, which God prepared in advance for us to do" (NIV). Ladies, when we fulfill our God-given purpose, we are gorgeous.

Of course, there is a balance here. We need to take care of our bodies, because if we believe in Christ, He lives in us. First Corinthians 6:19–20 says, "Do you not know that your body is a temple of the Holy Spirit, who is in you, whom you have received from God? You are not your own; you were bought at a price. Therefore honor God with your body" (NIV). Mistreating our bodies is like going into our church and writing graffiti all over the walls. Don't we want to treat our Father's house with respect?

However, that respect goes both ways. Just as we should exercise to build and maintain strength, and take in healthy food and drink to give our bodies fuel, we also shouldn't beat up on ourselves for becoming more wrinkled, hippy, or heavy as we age. That's simply how God designed women's bodies!

My writing buddy Sheila says, "At some point, we have to face the fact that our bodies were never meant to be permanent. They are disposable. How many times can you wash out a plastic bag before there are holes in it and you have to throw it away?"

Can you relate to that? Because whether we're smooth, wizened, jiggly, firm, tan, or pale, we are precious in His sight (to quote that wonderful children's song, "Jesus Loves Me").

And we are so much more than what shows on the outside. The most gorgeous women we know are stunning simply because they know who they are—and *whose* they are.

Now, if we can keep that belief front and center while the culture waves its you-must-be-perfect-to-be-loved/successful/beautiful flag all around us, we will have achieved something worthwhile.

But too many times we get lazy about what we let into our brains, and then reap the consequences. We must take care in this regard, for the things we read and watch—whether they're lies on the front of a tabloid magazine or the truth from God's Word—determine the state of our hearts.

The apostle Paul notes: "Therefore, since through God's mercy we have this ministry, we do not lose heart. Rather, we have renounced secret and shameful ways; we do not use deception, nor do we distort the word of God. On the contrary, by setting forth the truth plainly we commend ourselves to every man's conscience in the sight of God. . . . The god of this age has blinded the minds of unbelievers, so that they cannot see the light of the gospel of the glory of Christ, who is the image of God" (2 Corinthians 4:1–2, 4 NIV).

SETTING A COURSE

As Christian women, we need to not lose heart about our appearance, especially as we get older. Remember, Christ lives in us, and He is the image of God. The Bible says: "God saw all that he had made, and it was very good" (Genesis 1:31 NIV).

Author and speaker Margot Starbuck says, "When God made human beings, God looked at us and called us *very good*. It can be so tempting to believe the sinister hiss which insists, 'God *made* you good, but you messed it up,' or 'God made *others* good, but not you.' The fact is that God has called your body good. Believe it. Live into it."

She notes, "I'm a big talker when it comes to body image. I'm always spouting off about how women don't need to color our hair, or spend so much time on our faces, or tweak things surgically. In the occasional sane silent moment, I fear that when I get older I'll eat my well-intended words. I realize I may. My prayer is that as I lose hair pigmentation, and muscle tone, and experience other saggy situations, I'll be able to see myself through the eyes that see all of me and call me *good*."

When God sees us, He sees His daughters—His perfect, delightful, forgiven children. He doesn't see our pockmarked thighs.

We also need to renounce (and that means don't buy, read, watch, or support) the shameful ways of the world. We need to give up the gossip rags. Don't look at the tabloids or buy magazines that encourage unhealthy ways of living. Use discernment and prayerfully filter the junk that Hollywood churns out. We must watch where we surf on the Internet, and listen to uplifting radio programs.

It's so easy for us as women to get swept up in the craziness of the world. We long to be beautiful—and that's not a bad thing. God gave us that desire when He put us in the Garden. Our longing for beauty is a gift from our Father to make us pine for heaven. It's only unhealthy when we start beating up ourselves, and others, about being perfect. Perfection is not possible—at least not in this life.

Lane Jordan says, "To overcome our youth-driven culture, women need to focus each day on the Lord and support each other in every way they can. I just know that one day, I will be with Jesus and He promises to give me a brand-new body! That means no more wrinkles or cellulite!"

Amen! Let's put down the *Us Weekly* and pick up God's Word. When we immerse ourselves in His truth, we'll remember that God adores us, whether or not our arms are toned. He fancies us more than we can fathom, even though we might never have "abs of steel." He loves every single part of us, from the stretch marks on our bellies to the tiny dark hairs sprouting on our chins.

Even though we're plain jars of clay, He considers us His treasure. Look at what 2 Corinthians 4:7–12 says: "If you only look at us, you might well miss the brightness. We carry this precious Message around in the unadorned clay pots of our ordinary lives. That's to prevent anyone from confusing God's incomparable power with us. As it is, there's not much chance of that. You know for yourselves that we're not much to look at. We've been surrounded and battered by troubles, but we're not demoralized; we're not sure what to do, but we know that God knows what to do; we've been spiritually terrorized, but God hasn't left our side; we've been thrown down, but we haven't broken. What they did to Jesus, they do to us—trial and torture, mockery and murder; what Jesus did among them, He does in us—He lives! Our lives are at constant risk for Jesus' sake, which makes Jesus' life all the more evident in us. While we're going through the worst, you're getting in on the best!" (MSG).

Yes, we are getting older. That's life. There's a cycle at work that God put into place.

But even though we are dying, we have the life of Christ in us. His light in us can shine so much brighter than our flaws, if we'll let it. If we choose to die daily—not just physically, which is going to happen anyway, but spiritually, as in die to our own desires and will—then His life will flow through us to touch a hurting world with His grace. The Word says, "For we do not preach ourselves, but Jesus Christ as Lord, and ourselves as your servants for Jesus' sake. For God, who said, 'Let light shine out of darkness,' made his light shine in our hearts to give us the light of the knowledge of the glory of God in the face of Christ" (2 Corinthians 4:5–6 NIV).

As we deal with aching backs, ditzy brains, and deepening crow's-feet, we need to pray for God to make that overcoming, radiant spirit real in our lives. Because how we deal with our changing bodies affects the people around us, especially our kids.

Novelist Mary DeMuth noticed this recently as she puzzled over why her nearly-sixteen-year-old daughter had said, "Mom, you're pretty," so many times in the past few months. "To be honest," says Mary, "it was nice to hear, particularly as I head towards being twenty-one-twenty-one." But then she realized why Sophie was building her up: It was because Mary was not happy with her own reflection.

Mary says, "She will be insecure if I am insecure. She will reflect my own paranoia. She will get her attitude about how she looks by how I feel about how I look. If I'm stressing about extra pounds, chances are, she'll follow. So, in a roundabout way, her compliments served as a reminder to make peace with myself."

Mary, like many women, had been putting pressure on herself to have the same body (after bearing three children) as she did when she walked down the aisle as a toothpick-thin bride. But then she read Matthew 5:25 in a new way. It says, "Make friends quickly with your opponent at law while you are with him on the way, so that your opponent may not hand you over to the judge, and the judge to the officer, and you be thrown into prison" (NASB).

She realized she'd been guilty of not obeying that verse, only the opponent wasn't someone else—it was Mary. She notes, "I need to learn to make friends with my reflection, denying the nagging voice in my head. . .who compares me mercilessly to the latest teen heart throb. I am doing my daughters no favors by constantly worrying about my physique."

Mary's epiphany has prompted her to:

- Tell her daughter she is beautiful.
- Remind herself that God looks at the heart, and that her goal in life should be the beauty Jesus rewards, "the kind of heart that runs quickly to Him, full of mercy and patience and kindness."
- Shake hands with her forty-one-year-old self, realizing that she's healthy and happy.
- Defy the culture that glorifies youth and puts asunder anything less than perfection. Mary asks, "Is that what Jesus would do? Would He flock to the beautiful people? Since He created us all, we're all beautiful people. To place on each other this yoke of hierarchy is to discredit Jesus."
- Smile when she looks in the mirror, thankful for the years the Lord has given her. Because Mary's father died when she was young, she always thought she

would die in her thirties. "Well, I didn't," she admits. "And I'm so thankful!"

So, follow Mary's lead. As she says, "Give your family a gift today—make peace with your reflection. Glory in the body God has given you. Rejoice in the health you have. Trust that He will make your soul beautiful. And show the world this radical truth: a godly woman is content with how she looks."[2]

Along with letting God help us to be content with our appearance, we should also praise God for His gifts—first, people who love us no matter how we look, and second, laughter.

I'm so thankful that my hubby and two sons don't care what my measurements are. They love me simply because I'm me. In fact, they constantly tell me how nice I look. The other day, I woke up with some serious bed-hair. As I sat at my computer in a torn T-shirt and faded sweatpants, my sweet, thoughtful, and obviously vision-impaired four-year-old said, "Mommy, you're pretty in your day clothes, your pajamas, or even on a date."

That perspective is a gift, as are the humorous moments that aging brings into our lives. Let's face it, sometimes the only way to deal with the changes getting older brings is to laugh at them! Case in point: Christine was in a diner with her husband and two children when she noticed a younger,

---

[2] See relevantblog.blogspot.com/2008/11/my-body-image-my-daughter.html. Used with permission.

good-looking male staring at her. She began to feel flirty, thinking the young man found her attractive.

Yes, I still have it! she thought. But as the family got up to leave, her son pulled at her arm and said, "Mom, you have ketchup on your nose!"

Those kinds of moments can embarrass us, and make us groan. Let's be honest—we groan a lot as we age. We groan when we get up, when we sit down, and when we're doing nothing.

Did you know God's Word addresses even this? Check this out: "Now we know that if the earthly tent we live in is destroyed, we have a building from God, an eternal house in heaven, not built by human hands. Meanwhile we groan, longing to be clothed with our heavenly dwelling, because when we are clothed, we will not be found naked. For while we are in this tent, we groan and are burdened, because we do not wish to be unclothed but to be clothed with our heavenly dwelling, so that what is mortal may be swallowed up by life" (2 Corinthians 5:1–4 NIV).

What Paul is saying is that even as our earthly bodies are being destroyed, if we believe in Jesus, we have an eternal body that can never die. And our aging process can turn us toward and not away from God—if we'll let it.

And how do we do that? We trust in God, by His spirit, to work His purposes in our lives: "Now it is God who has made us for this very purpose and has given us the Spirit as a deposit, guaranteeing what is to come"(2 Corinthians 5:5 NIV).

Paul goes on to say that as we daily walk by faith and not by sight, we can be confident. We can know beyond a doubt that God is perfecting us spiritually, even as gravity and our decaying cells destroy us physically. And we make it our goal to please Him, not the masses of people who want to sell us eternal youth: "Therefore we are always confident and know that as long as we are at home in the body we are away from the Lord. We live by faith, not by sight. We are confident, I say, and would prefer to be away from the body and at home with the Lord. So we make it our goal to please him, whether we are at home in the body or away from it" (2 Corinthians 5:6–9 NIV).

It's simple, but not easy. We must continually look heavenward, and not get swept up in the madness that surrounds us. When we do that, we are changed. . .and we also bless others.

Margot Starbuck says, "I love to see an older woman who's not trying to hide anything, or cover it up, or firm it, or lift it, or reshape it. When I'm walking on the beach, or through town, I like to look into women's faces and search for the ones who are simply satisfied with who they are. In contrast to those of us who are doing all the squeezing and coloring and hoisting, these truly liberated women are like a breath of fresh air."

Margot believes that as we age, we have the power to bless

others if we do it well: "By 'well' I mean that we don't buy into the world's priorities which devalue those who are older. When we choose to love ourselves the way God loves us, we break the power that binds us and so many others. As other women look to us, noticing us choosing to live lives of love, they are freed up to be the women God made them to be. We *have* that power."

She also believes that another way to break the power that holds us hostage to the importance of appearances is to express gratitude to God. She says, "Why not give thanks not for how our bodies *appear*, but rather for what they are able to *do*? I'm not talking about competing in marathons or skydiving, either. We break the power of the culture's insistence on physical attractiveness when we thank God for bodies that do what they were made to do, like feeling the sun and wind on our skin, walking with a friend, tasting sweet juicy peaches, or having the strength to hold a baby."

Now that's something we can squeeze into.

SMOOTH SAILING

Have you been swept up in the appearance-driven media culture? Has the mirror become your biggest enemy? If so, resolve to stop listening to disparaging voices and worldly influences. Instead, saturate yourself with the Word of God, and remember that God cares more about the size of your heart than the size of your jeans. Really!

As you look around you, notice the women who are aging well. Are they beautiful only on the outside? Of course not! They glow because they have accepted themselves fully. As they sail through the accumulating years, they enjoy the feel of the winds of change on their faces (at least most of the time!). These women, secure in their heritage as daughters of the King, determine to "do" getting older gracefully, despite the aches and pains it brings. They give thanks for the ways their bodies can still move, and they look for the lighthouse of God's truth on every corner.

Because they spend time fellowshipping with God, ignoring the world's lies, and surrounding themselves with like-minded women, they are radiant.

If you long to become like them, try placing these verses on index cards and taping them to all the mirrors in your house. Digest the words, and savor them throughout the day. Hold on to them as if they were life preservers, and you're a sailor on a boat, in the midst of a huge storm. The Word of

God gives life, and His truth *will* set you free!

- *"God sees not as a man sees, for man looks at the outward appearance, but the LORD looks at the heart."*
  1 SAMUEL 16:7 NASB

- *The silver-haired head is a crown of glory, if it is found in the way of righteousness.*
  PROVERBS 16:31 NKJV

- *"Steep yourself in God-reality, God-initiative, God-provisions. You'll find all your everyday human concerns will be met."*
  LUKE 12:31 MSG

- *"For my thoughts are not your thoughts, neither are your ways my ways," declares the LORD. "As the heavens are higher than the earth, so are my ways higher than your ways and my thoughts than your thoughts."*
  ISAIAH 55: 8–9 NIV

Chapter 3

MAKE THE MOST OF WHAT YOU'VE GOT

In a man's middle years there is scarcely a part of the body he would hesitate to turn over to the proper authorities.
E. B. WHITE

THE DRIFT

Many of us have a love-hate relationship with exercise. We love what it does for us, and we hate actually doing it.

Once we stop growing upward and instead grow outward, we may make a resolution to get in shape. Then, as we begin running or doing high-impact aerobics, following videos or training at a gym, we may begin to develop some physical problems—strained knees, sore shoulders, backaches, etc. As a result, we may start exercising infrequently, or perhaps give it up altogether. Even if we eventually get back into daily workouts, we may get bored easily, never sticking with any one exercise for very long.

We're not alone in our struggle. Remember Oprah? Because of heart palpitations due to a thyroid problem and hormonal imbalance, she stopped exercising, took herself off her list of priorities in 2007, and had the weight gain—and regrets—to prove it. She said she stopped doing the things she knew were good for her—because she tried to do too much for everyone else. And as stress piled on top of stress, her body began to rebel.

Most of us can relate to putting our needs last on the list. As women, we tend to take care of everyone else first. We love to nurture people, and that doesn't always include ourselves.

Last fall, I began feeling the effects of too many months of self-neglect. Since having mono in 1995 at the age of twenty-five, I have struggled with autoimmune issues, including chronic fatigue, hypothyroidism, depression, food allergies, and more. Some days have been better than others, but it's been quite a roller-coaster ride as I've tried to find doctors who would give me answers (and not just prescriptions). Having two kids along the way was a blessing, but it complicated my health issues, to say the least. And as the years tick away, I've begun to experience lots of female problems, as well.

After a bout of shingles last fall, I began sliding into a severe depression again, which made every day a struggle. So, with the encouragement of my sweet, patient hubby, we began searching for a doctor in our area who could help. My previous doctor was awesome—but five hours away was just too far.

We prayed, did online searches, looked at insurance information, and then God led me to Dr. Ruthie Harper. She's an MD who found that her patients' lives changed dramatically for the better when she began combining nutrition, supplements, and other "alternative" treatments with more conventional methods. So after extensive blood work and questions about my medical history, Dr. Harper changed my diet and put me on several supplements, as well as bioidentical hormones. She also recommended "calming exercise," which is great, because I enjoy yoga and love walks with my friend. Those are kinds of exercise I can live with!

And although I'm definitely not recommending this approach for everyone—or even *most* women—it really worked for me, making every day of my life better!

What about you? What changes are you experiencing in your health? Do you have hot flashes, headaches, and trouble sleeping? Perhaps your knees are giving out from too many years of abuse. Maybe your back is yelling at you for not taking care of it during your earlier decades. Or, more frightening, perhaps you've received a scary diagnosis of diabetes, hypertension, or cancer.

If so, you're in good company. Every one of us faces the fact of our body giving out on us after we hit a certain age. As my late grandma used to say, "After forty, it's just patch, patch, patch!"

Forty-something Janelle is facing chemo, radiation, and surgery after a doctor found a lump in her breast. She wonders if she has what it takes to endure the next few months. She's divorced, and is afraid of losing her job and her home, in addition to her health.

Fifty-five-year-old Nia has to start exercising and eating better because her doctor told her that her cholesterol is at dangerous levels. She doesn't know if she has the discipline or knowledge to eat right. Her husband has his own set of problems, and their kids have a lot of issues, as well. She questions whether or not she can follow through with a new routine when her life is so busy and chaotic.

And Savannah, who's in her sixties, deals with fibromyalgia and chronic fatigue. She has trouble getting up each morning, and her pain is sometimes unbearable. She knows she should exercise, but it takes all her energy just to make it through the day. As a widow, she feels alone, especially because her grown children live three states away.

BALLAST

Whatever the health challenges we're facing, we have God's peace as an anchor. Remember that He promises to be with us, whatever we're going through. Psalm 29:11 says, "The LORD gives strength to his people; the LORD blesses his people with peace" (NIV). And though we need to accept that our bodies will change as we age, that doesn't mean we need to throw our hands up in the air and say, "Oh, well. I'm going to get old anyway, so it doesn't matter what I do." Instead, we need to take care of what we've got. Remember, God gives us choices, and those little choices add up to big changes (for good or bad) in the quality of our lives.

First Corinthians 10:23 says, " 'Everything is permissible'—but not everything is beneficial. 'Everything is permissible'—but not everything is constructive" (NIV). Paul's talking to the church in Corinth about the law, saying that because of Jesus, we don't have to follow the Old Testament rules about what's okay to eat and what's not. But he's also telling the Corinthians that just because we *can* do something doesn't always mean we *should*. It's reminiscent of what Jeff Goldblum's character said to the dinosaur theme–park creator in the flick *Jurassic Park*: "You were so busy worrying about whether you could, you didn't stop to think about whether you should."

That's a good rule to follow about eating, too. We don't want to eat anything under the sun, just because we can. Our bodies were meant to run a certain way, and they do best when we give them the best fuel. We're all busy, and it does take time, planning, and discipline to put the right stuff in our mouths. But it's also worth it!

God created life as a cycle, and we will die, that's true. But God also created our bodies as amazing, interconnected "machines." The choices we make with regard to eating, exercise, and stress management will affect not only our physical health but also our mental, emotional, and spiritual health.

Leslie Wilson says her biggest concern about getting older is not being able to keep up with her kids and (someday) grandkids. However, she also admits that her fear has lately been a good thing. She says, "In the past year and a half, I've lost twenty pounds, joined a gym, and completed a triathlon. If I don't want aging to keep me from doing things with my younger family members, I need to be actively doing something about its effects on my physical body. I stretch well, work out hard—cardio and weights, as well as fast-walking or bike riding—and eat fairly well. (I could never deny myself that egg roll or delicious dark chocolate.)"

We can applaud Leslie for taking care of her body before health problems pop up. So, what can *we* do to make the most of what we've got?

> **First, realize that you can't ignore your health without severe repercussions.** God has set up our bodies with warning signals, and I encourage you not to ignore those signals when they come. If you know you're doing something (drinking heavily, smoking, eating tons of junk food) that is detrimental to your physical well-being, ask God for the strength to stop. If you have Christ in your heart, He has already given you self-control—it's one of the fruits of the Spirit! "But the fruit of the Spirit is love, joy, peace, patience, kindness, goodness, faithfulness, gentleness and self-control. Against such things there is no law" (Galatians 5:22–23 NIV).
>
> **Listen to your body; you know it better than anyone else.** Please, please, if you have unexplained pain, fatigue, strange bruises or spots, or any number of other symptoms, get to a doctor. And don't stop with

the first physician, either, if his or her diagnosis doesn't jive with your symptoms, instincts, or experience.

When we listen to a doctor and follow his/her advice without thinking or researching all our options, it can do more harm than good. Each of us was created unique by God, and that means there is no one lifestyle that will fit everyone. The diet that works for you may be terrible for me. We need to listen to our bodies and respond in the best way for us. Pray about the health-care decisions you make—God cares about all areas of our lives, not just the spiritual aspects.

Your health affects every other area of your life. When our health is good, everything feels better—mind, spirit, and body. When we're struggling with health issues, it colors the rest of our lives, too. That's why it's so important to take care of ourselves. In addition, as we discussed in the last chapter, our body is the temple of God. We need to be good stewards of it.

When Carol hit the age of fifty, she suddenly lost interest in sex (we'll talk more about this in the next chapter). Throughout the day, she would think, *Tonight's the night.* But when nighttime rolled around, all she wanted to do was go to sleep. She says, "Fortunately, I had a really sweet and understanding husband who never pressured me in any way." She went to several doctors, and each one prescribed something different. But, in the end, what Carol discovered was that she was just plain tired.

Carol says, "I finally learned I had to honor God by taking care of this body He blessed me with. I have slowly begun to recognize that when I am tired physically or mentally, it affects every aspect of my life."

There are many things you can't control—but many that you can. Yes, we're going to get wrinkles, and our bodies will have aches and pains as we get older. We can't always control what diseases we might get, or keep ourselves from getting sick. But over and over again, science has shown that many problems can be prevented by avoiding excessive sugar and alcohol, eating whole grains and lean proteins, ingesting lots of fruits and veggies, drinking mostly water instead of sugary and caffeinated drinks, and limiting our intake of processed/refined foods.

You don't have to do everything. We want to take care of everyone else. But when we run until we can't run anymore, we don't give our bodies the balance they crave. It's so easy to say yes to everything we're asked to participate in. But we need to learn how to say no and be more mindful about the choices we make.

You need your "Sabbath" rest. Remember that only God can take care of everyone—and even He needed rest! That's why He created the Sabbath and rested from His work on the seventh day. He knew we needed rest, too—and even commanded it. Exodus 20:8 says, "Observe the Sabbath day, to keep it holy. Work six days and do everything you need to do. But the seventh day is a Sabbath to GOD, your God. Don't do any work—not you, nor your son, nor your daughter, nor your servant, nor your maid, nor your animals, not even the foreign guest visiting in your town. For in six days GOD made Heaven, Earth, and sea, and everything in them; he rested on the seventh day. Therefore GOD blessed the Sabbath day; he set it apart as a holy day" (MSG).

So, regularly give yourself a break—if not for your sake, then for all those people (family, friends, boss, co-workers) who count on you every day. Give yourself permission to be human. Make time for you. Take a bubble bath; read an uplifting book; watch a great movie; call a friend; play with your dog; take a nap. And be sure and take longer breaks once or twice a year. The American Journal of Epidemiology followed people for twenty years and found that those who took frequent vacations decreased their heart attack risk by 50 percent.[3] Wow! Think you can't afford a vacation? Swap homes with a friend in a

---

[3] Eaker, Elaine D., Joan Pinsky, and William P. Castelli. "Myocardial Infarction and Coronary Death among Women: Psychosocial Predictors from a 20-Year Follow-up of Women in the Framingham Study." *American Journal of Epidemiology* 135.8 (1992): 854–64.

resort town, do a "stay-cation" in your hometown, or barter services for downtime. Whatever it takes, just do it!

Remember what it's like to feel bad—especially when you feel good. During the times our health is good, we need to remember the choices that helped us feel that way. It's so easy to go back to old habits and think, *This won't hurt me.* Think you don't have time or money to exercise or eat right? Sure, it can be tough. But just think of it this way: If you mistreat your body by not doing the right things, you'll end up paying a lot more later, either with doctor bills, medicine, lost work time—or all three.

Mina Delgado is a busy forty-something mom of a toddler. She says, "I don't have the same body I used to, but for the most part, I feel fantastic. I had my son at forty-one. Now that he's almost three, I can't seem to find the time to regularly work out, so I get on the floor and do my crunches. As soon as my son sees me doing exercise, he runs to get the exercise ball and plops it on my stomach. He then joins me and tries to do the exercises himself. Just the other night my husband said, 'Wow, I was looking at pictures of you before the baby. You still look great!' I thank God every day for helping me stay as fit as I can despite not getting as much exercise. (You try running after a two-and-a-half-year-old baby boy and see if you don't stay fit!)"

Why not follow Mina's lead and try to incorporate exercise into your day? If you struggle with fatigue, you may find it hard to believe that exercising is better for you than resting, and that exercise actually gives energy to the body. It also provides oxygen to your brain and tissues (which means more mental clarity and stamina throughout the day) and releases endorphins, which help you feel better emotionally.

You don't have to join a gym—instead, pop in an exercise video or walk the dog around your block. Or find a free workout video online. Even ten minutes a day will give you health benefits. And don't forget to stretch—it increases your flexibility and can help you avoid injuries. It's especially important to stretch daily as you get older.

Join a support group. Do you long to drop pounds or add regular exercise to your routine but hate going it alone? Does the thought of quitting smoking terrify you, because you've tried before (numerous times) and failed? Whether you're dealing with cancer, thyroid conditions, or a host of other symptoms, there is a support group for you—whether locally or in cyberspace (or both).

The Bible tells us that meeting together is a vital part of building godly community: "Let us not give up meeting together, as some are in the habit of doing, but let us encourage one another—and all the more as you see the Day approaching" (Hebrews 10:25 NIV).

Your church may have a group that fits your needs. And don't overlook the local Yellow Pages. Who knows where you'll find like-minded, genuine, caring friends who can help shoulder your load? If you can't locate a group in your area, look up your health problem on the Internet, and find a Web site with a discussion forum or an e-mail support group you can join. Just having people who understand the intricacies of your condition will help you feel better. You can cry, complain, and rant—without feeling judged.

Learn to embrace solitude. So many of us are afraid of being alone—especially as we age. And with many women living longer than men, ending up alone is a valid concern. But solitude doesn't have to be scary. In fact, it can become a gift.

Personally, I crave solitude but am very unlikely to just "happen upon" it—even in the bathroom. But that's okay. I've learned to carve out time for myself by being creative and diligent.

Maybe you have all the alone time you could want. . .and then some. Or maybe you're like Ruby and Anna, two women who have equally challenging, if different, schedules. Ruby is an executive's wife whose husband is "always underfoot." She lives in a wealthy subdivision in a resort community. Her days are filled with tennis lessons, charity board meetings, errands with and for her husband, and shopping. Time alone? Ha! Anna is a single mom who works as a secretary and a part-time piano instructor. Her days are filled shuttling her two teenagers to and from school and activities, working, and home maintenance. Time alone? Not likely.

You may find it almost impossible to carve out time for yourself. And yet, whether we realize it or not, we each need a daily pocket of time to call our own. (Yes, even outgoing women can find serenity, hope, and a renewed sense of creativity after being alone.)

Why? Solitude replenishes and refreshes us. It's a necessary, and often overlooked, facet of a restful, balanced life. American women are great at forgetting to enjoy life. Instead, we stay connected to the Internet or our Blackberries (or old-fashioned cell phones) and multitask away our days. We choose to let our schedules run us, instead of us running our schedules. And we get so wrapped up in trying to keep up with what other people are doing that we forget to look up and ask God what we should be doing.

Only cats have nine lives. We have but one. And it is a supermyth that you can be Superwoman. In fact, you can do some of it, and have some of it done, but if you try to do it all, you'll be done in.

And finally, we can see from God's heavenly perspective and:

Learn to embrace suffering. I pray that God will allow us to make the necessary mental and spiritual adjustments so we can begin to thank God daily for the sufferings we experience as we age. With His help, we can choose to see the tough things we're going through as a purifier of our fleshly nature: "Therefore we do not lose heart. Though outwardly we are wasting away, yet inwardly we are being renewed day by day. For our light and momentary troubles are achieving for us an eternal glory that far outweighs them all. So we fix our eyes not on what is seen, but on what is unseen. For what is seen is temporary, but what is unseen is eternal" (2 Corinthians 4:16–18 NIV).

What we can see—our wrinkles, sagging skin, and various other "flaws"—is nothing compared to the faith, wisdom, and beauty God is building in us as we sail with Him through the sea of changes. Ladies, because of Him, we have hope. . .not in ourselves, but in Christ. We shouldn't look to the mirror for our worth, or consider the stars to tell us our future. We know without a doubt that our bodies will eventually die, but we also know that if we trust in Christ, we will live forever. That's good news, and it's worth shouting from the rooftops!

In the New Testament, Peter wrote: "Blessed be the God and Father of our Lord Jesus Christ, who according to His great mercy has caused us to be born again to a living hope through the resurrection of Jesus Christ from the dead, to obtain an inheritance which is imperishable and undefiled and will not fade away, reserved in heaven for you, who are protected by the power of God through faith for a salvation ready to be revealed in the last time" (1 Peter 1:3–5 NASB).

Ladies, God's great mercy gave us this promise and protection. We have a reservation—not for an elegant spa, which will help us fade our age spots—but for eternal bliss, which will never fade away. In heaven, we won't be sick or weak or imperfect in any way. Now if that doesn't give your face (and heart) a lift, I don't know what will!

Peter also wrote: "In this you greatly rejoice, even though now for a little while, if necessary, you have been distressed by various trials, so that the proof of your faith, being more precious than gold which is perishable, even though tested by fire, may be found to result in praise and glory and honor at the revelation of Jesus Christ" (1 Peter 1:6–7 NASB).

Whether we believe it or not, God can use all the worst things about aging—the uncertainties, illnesses, memory lapses, and losses—to purify our hearts, if we'll let Him. He wants to comfort us in those trials so that we can comfort others. When we take our complaints and concerns to Him in honesty and transparency, He will give us His presence and peace, and we, in turn, can give that peace to others we come in contact with. In this way, we're giving glory to Him, and that will result in praise and honor for Jesus.

Author Marcia Lee Laycock was crushed the day her optometrist told her she needed bifocals. "Friends had warned me this day would come. After a few days of feeling like I was on drugs, I got used to the things and tried to dismiss the fact that I had just passed a telltale milestone. But I kept having dreams where strangers would gleefully yell: 'Aha! You wear bifocals. We know how old you are!' Eventually, I relaxed in the world of thousands who peer through lenses with a line across the bottom."

Three years later, she inadvertently crushed her glasses. She relates, "The sound of the frames snapping was quite satisfying. But it was time for another eye examination anyway. I was prepared to hear that my eyes had weakened. I was not prepared for the doctor to tell me I needed trifocals.

He advised I switch to a progressive lens."

So Marcia put them on and peered at the world. Everything was blurry at first. Marcia's doctor told her to swivel her whole head, not just her eyes. And she says, "The results were wonderful. I could see clearly at any distance. And I have resigned myself to the fact that at my age, to see clearly I need a little help."[4]

We all need help seeing clearly—especially spiritually. God's brand of bifocals (and trifocals, if you will) is His Word. As we train ourselves to consider His truth, the devil's lies come more into focus. And the benefits of living His way—and not the world's—become clear.

Millie McNabb has God's perspective on getting older. When she was a teenager with long blond hair, Millie read Proverbs 16:31: "Gray hair is a crown of splendor; it is attained by a righteous life" (NIV). She was attracted to that concept and made a commitment at that time to not dye her hair, as well as to live a righteous life. She says, "Over the years, I watched the 'gray-headed' women at church gatherings, and appreciated their wisdom. And when I was in my forties, God sent me a little test as my hair started to gray. In the course of one week, three people—my hairdresser, my husband, and my mother-in-law—independently asked me if I'd ever considered dying my hair. But I kept to my youthful commitment and have never dyed my hair."

---

[4] Laycock, Marcia Lee. "The Trick to Seeing Clearly" devotional. Used with permission. For more information, see www.vinemarc.com.

Millie notes that gray hair does have its advantages in the senior-discount area: "I would tell the clerk that I didn't qualify, and they'd be so embarrassed at their error, that they'd give me the discount anyway."

Millie has also been inspired by Deuteronomy 34:7: "Although Moses was one hundred and twenty years old when he died, his eye was not dim, nor his vigor abated" (NASB).

Millie believes that you don't have to be diseased, just because you are getting older. After much reading about being healthy, she came to the conclusion that she should not waste her time on trying to keep up with the world's changing philosophies on health, aging, and disease, but rather rely on what the Bible says about how to eat.[5]

What about you? What is your perspective on aging? I hope you're beginning to see it as not something to be endured, but rather enjoyed and even—yes!—celebrated.

So much of aging well is about our attitude. Why not set a goal to be like eighty-one-year-old Myrtle, who says, "I don't feel very old"?

Myrtle loves Joshua 13, in which God speaks to Joshua, who He describes as "old and stricken in years" (Joshua 13:1 KJV) and says, "there remains very much land yet to be possessed" (Joshua 13:1 NKJV). She also notes that an eighty-five-year-old Caleb tells Joshua that he was forty when Moses sent him to spy out the Promised Land. And now, forty-five

---

[5] From personal interview with Millie McNabb; see www.ChristianValuesLegacy.com for more information.

years later, Caleb says, "I am as strong this day as on the day that Moses sent me; just as my strength was then, so now is my strength for. . .going out and for coming in" (Joshua 14:11 NKJV)! That's a true testimony of longevity and God's strength sustaining His servants for the long haul.

"God has been good to me and I feel like I still have a lot of 'get up and go'—and some more land to possess. I pray I will do whatever it is He has for me before I complete my days on earth," Myrtle concludes.

SMOOTH SAILING

What health issues do you face? Have you made peace with them, or are you searching for answers? Know that whatever God has placed in your life, He has plans to prosper you and not harm you, to give you hope and a future (Jeremiah 29:11).

And change what you can. Take charge of your health! You're the best advocate you have. Get enough rest, and don't work too hard. Resolve to worry less and pray more. If you're not exercising, start today. Quit those bad habits, and replace them with healthier ones. Meet with like-minded folks for support and accountability. And spend time alone, to refresh yourself as well as hear from the Lord. By hearing from Him and basking in His presence, you can begin to embrace the hard things as a way to look more like Him. Do all these things for your family and friends, if not for yourself (and the Lord). Remember, He is with you, and He is for you!

Jot these scriptures down where you can see them throughout the week, and find a partner to memorize them with. Call each other (or e-mail) as you go about your busy lives, reminding each other to focus on the eternal instead of the temporary.

- *"He will renew your life and sustain you in your old age."*
  RUTH 4:15 NIV

- *"You will go out in joy and be led forth in peace; the mountains and hills will burst into song before you, and all the trees of the field will clap their hands."*
  ISAIAH 55:12 NIV

- *"Work six days. The seventh day is a Sabbath, a day of total and complete rest, a sacred assembly. Don't do any work. Wherever you live, it is a Sabbath to GOD."*
  LEVITICUS 23:3 MSG

- *"Shout that people are like the grass. Their beauty fades as quickly as the flowers in a field. The grass withers and the flowers fade beneath the breath of the LORD. And so it is with people. The grass withers and the flowers fade, but the word of our God stands forever."*
  ISAIAH 40:6–8 NLT

Chapter 4

Love Out Loud

THE SENILITY PRAYER
Grant me the senility to forget the
people I never liked anyway,
the good fortune to run into the ones I do,
and the eyesight to tell the difference.
UNKNOWN

THE DRIFT

Relationships are not easy, and though they can be richer, deeper, and more satisfying as the years go by, getting older also brings with it difficulties in dealing with others—whether they're meddling in-laws, set-in-their-ways spouses, adult children with shaky finances, or finicky friends. Hormones and physical changes bring about one set of challenges. Memory lapses, fatigue, and hurts from the past cause other issues to crop up.

Take this example: As child rearing winds down, your adventure-loving mate longs to travel together in an RV and discover all the hidden corners of the United States. You, on the other hand, breathe a sigh of relief because the kids are gone and you can finally have some alone time. But when you were first married, you were the adventurous one who couldn't wait to be together, and he was the homebody who needed space. *What has changed?* you wonder. *And is it okay? Just how much change is too much?*

Or say you're a single woman with a thriving career, but no hubby or kids. You're happy, healthy, and feel blessed to get to travel and do something you love. Yet, each holiday, you endure questions from well-meaning relatives about your "ticking clock" and how "you'll regret not having children." Then there's Aunt Polly, who has asked you every Thanksgiving—since college!—if you have a special guy in your life. It's enough to make a grown woman scream, leave a family gathering, and order in Chinese food for Christmas!

Every relationship goes through stages of growth and change. They're much like a sailing trip in a small vessel. When the weather is great, it's gorgeous, and you wouldn't want to be anywhere else. But when a storm hits, your journey consists of thrills and chills, with a few vomit-inducing and terrifying moments thrown in for good measure.

Each stage of your relationships will have different joys, challenges, and opportunities. Whether you've known the person for two, ten, or twenty-five years, you never know what's around the next bend. What matters most is your attitude—and that you're in this thing called "life" together. So grab that cotton candy and hold on. . .you're in for the adventure of a lifetime!

Recognizing that every person who joins with another person in the adventure of friendship or family life is flawed can help us as we ride life's waves.

Here are the stages we often go through with loved ones:

The honeymoon stage.

During the honeymoon phase, which can last from a few weeks to several years, you see only the good in each other. *What a lovely mother-in-law!* you think—until she starts criticizing your housekeeping. "I have the perfect child," you believe—until the first tantrum. And just before your second husband has unpacked his things in your house—arranging his clothes *his* way, not yours!—you look into his eyes and sigh, "You're amazing. No flaws."

Relish the honeymoon stage of relationships (because it won't last forever) by recording your feelings in a journal. Later, you can read your entries when the going inevitably gets tough.

In my marriage, most of our arguments have stemmed from our rather basic differences in personality. He's a neat freak, and I'm only neat behind cabinet doors. He's thorough and detailed, and I think that's boring and takes too much time. He's an extrovert; I'm an introvert.

Over the years, we've learned to accept and appreciate our differences (thankfully, or we would have killed each other!). So first,

- *Consider your loved one's personality—and yours.* You'll be amazed at how you'll grow in understanding of people if you invest in a book or course on that subject. It's truly life-changing!
- *Find mentors.* The second way to keep relationships on an even keel during the honeymoon stage is to look for mentors. One of the best things my husband and I ever did was to find an older couple to model our marriage after (we hung out with them and asked

questions). They were sweet, loving, fun, and very much in love. In their golden years, they traveled, went Texas two-stepping, and enjoyed their kids and grandkids. Ruthie and George modeled a mature, godly love for us. We soaked up their friendship as much as possible before we moved away from them.

If you're single, invite an older godly single woman to lunch. Ask her questions about the relationships she's had—familial or otherwise—and see what you can glean from her hard-earned wisdom.

- *Put up hedges of protection.* As a newly married couple, my husband and I didn't want others to encroach too much on our life, especially when we were starting out. If you're a single mom, be sure and do this with your kids, protecting that one-on-one time with them. If in-laws or other people want to stay with you for long periods of time, give you frequent advice, or ask questions that make you uncomfortable, be firm but polite in setting limits.
- *Put Jesus first.* If worship and fellowship are a part of your life, your decisions, priorities, and schedules will fall into place.

Those four steps can help anyone, in any relationship, thrive when the honeymoon stage ends.

The big adjustment.

The next phase of a relationship occurs from several weeks to several years after the relationship begins, and can last for a decade or more. It's called the "big adjustment." Seemingly overnight, you begin to see all the flaws you had ignored before, and miniscule things start to bug the fire out of you.

Still, while there are difficulties in leaving the honeymoon phase behind, there are also real perks to the big adjustment. For in this latter stage, most people find a new level of comfort and authenticity in their relationship now that the "honeymoon" is over.

Ladies, if you learn to serve your friends and family members—parents, in-laws, outlaws—and see them as God sees them (not perfect, but delightful and distinct children of the King) during this phase, you'll have many opportunities for growth. And as we grow, we'll begin to understand better not only how to love but also how to be loved. And it's sad, but true: During this second phase, when it applies to marriage, many couples give up and divorce.

And if you've been there—I am so sorry. Whatever the circumstances surrounding your divorce, I pray God will touch you with His healing hand and restore your joy and hope.

The Bible says that God hates divorce. (Notice I didn't say "God hates *divorcees.*" That's a crucial difference!) Why? He abhors what it does to families and children. He created marriage to be a lifelong commitment, in which two people spend the time and energy getting to know each other through all the different stages of life.

As I write this, a dear friend is going through a divorce. Her husband cheated on her, but she was the one who filed for the legal action. And that's when things got really ugly. He is now fighting her for custody of their two children—even though he's the one who abandoned his family. I encouraged her that she was a good mother, and with tears in her eyes, she replied, "It's sad that a court has to decide that now."

Of course, God can heal and redeem a sad situation. I've seen that, too—over and over, in fact. Sometimes, second marriages are God's greatest gift to people who've been walked over and wrung out.

But God's ideal is that a couple stays together "for better, for worse, till death do us part." That's why the vows we speak in our marriage ceremony are so vital, so crucial, to the relationship. They're not suggestions, or things we do when we feel like it. They are sacred promises to honor and prefer another human being over ourselves—to serve our spouse as Christ served His disciples. A friend's therapist said once, to her and her husband as they went through counseling: "I don't love my wife every day, but I am committed to her every day."

Sometimes you may not feel loving toward a spouse, friend, or family member—but that doesn't mean you can't *act* loving. Here are a few ideas to get you started:

LOVE OUT LOUD

- *Pray.* Pray with your loved one whenever you can. Even if the person (your friend, child, parent, or other family member) isn't comfortable praying with you, ask for specific requests so you each pray on your own. (You can also make a journal of your prayers and God's answers. Later, you can surprise that person with a copy of the journal—where you've recorded needs and answers—as a meaningful gift.) And if your loved one isn't a believer, or doesn't attend church with you, pray for your loved one as you stand for Christ alone. And remember, He is with you, so you're not really alone!

  One effective and transforming way to pray is to take scripture and adapt it to your loved one's needs. The Word of God is full of verses that you can use almost word-for-word as personal, practical prayers.
- *Share.* Share burdens by asking questions, especially when the person appears stressed out, and by listening. Sometimes just getting things off our chest helps us feel calmer. And share in your loved one's hobbies and activities when it's appropriate. Just be careful to give him or her enough space—especially if the individual is an introvert.
- *Give.* The most important gift you can give people is encouragement. Tell them what you love about them, especially when they are down. Write a letter,

thanking them for the things they have done for you.

Or try to give of your talents by baking their favorite treats or by making a CD of uplifting music—including some by you, if you're gifted in that area—they can play in the car or on the computer.

Whatever you choose to do, know that God will honor your desire to support your loved one. As Proverbs 11:25 says, "He [or she!] who refreshes others will himself be refreshed" (NIV). So ask the Lord for creative ideas, and implement them with prayer, patience, and persistence. If you're faithful to minister to your friends and family members, I guarantee you *will* see refreshment.

It's unfortunate, but during this second phase of life together, people can get complacent and begin to take their loved one for granted.

That's why God gave us His strength, His grace, and His commitment. "Doing life" with other people brings us to our knees. It tests our endurance and patience. We say, "I give up! It's too hard! I can't do it!" and God says, *"Good. I was waiting for you to say that. Now let Me do it through you."*

And He will, if we'll let Him. With His help, loved ones can make each other a priority.

One thing my husband, Carey, and I've done during this phase of marriage is rely on others when things got really messy. Two different times, we've gone to counseling.

It wasn't easy, but it was one of the best things we ever did for our relationship. If you have a series of ugly fights with a parent, child, or other relative, and don't know how to change the pattern, a pastor or godly counselor can help. Don't feel ashamed about asking—even good relationships need assistance once in a while.

The committed phase.

This third phase begins when people with different backgrounds, emotions, and personalities settle into their roles and find a comfort level that they both enjoy.

It's not without its stresses, though. If you're in the committed phase and things are going great with you and your husband, you might be experiencing hot flashes while your teenager is dealing with acne and a breakup with her boyfriend. Perhaps you are single, and your friends and relatives are all raising children, so you have less in common. Maybe you're a widow and your energy (not to mention your budget) is stressed to the limit by car payments, insurance premiums, and rent, and at the same time, you're trying to decide whether or not to have home health care look in on your parents, who live across the country. You want to keep your commitment to honor your parents, as God requires, but you feel overwhelmed. And keeping commitments—unspoken or implied—to your friends? That seems simply impossible.

As some of us become part of the "sandwich generation"—daily dealing with our kids (some who have moved back in to live with Mom and Dad after not being able to find a well-paying job) and our aging parents—the stress fractures that pop up can splinter even the healthiest relationships.

During the stressful times, remember:

- *God is constant and perfect, and your loved one is not.*
- *Emotionally draining seasons will come, but they will also eventually leave.*
- *And for goodness' sake, laugh as much as possible! If you can laugh about life, you can roll with the punches much more easily.*

Older but wiser.

Marriages move into this older-but-wiser stage when children are grown and leave home. Bonds with children and parents deepen in this final stage, when surface issues no longer threaten to derail your commitment to one another.

On the positive side of the coin, older-but-wiser people have the opportunity to reconnect. They sometimes have more freedom in their schedule and more money to play with. Carol says, "This is a wonderful time in my life. Our adult children are happy, successful, and self sufficient! My husband and I love this stage. The flexibility to do whatever we want, whenever we want, is liberating. We have no one else's schedule to consult. No sports schedules, no school calendars, no birthday parties to plan! We just do whatever we want and look forward to the visits from the adults who will always be 'our children.' And we look forward to grandchildren (even if that means sports schedules, birthday parties, etc.)!"

Another benefit of the older-but-wiser stage for those who are married is that there's more opportunity for physical intimacy, with a quiet house and more experience.

My marriage mentor, Ruthie, says, "I wouldn't trade any part of our marriage of fifty years for the part we're in right now. Not the months of adjustments following the wedding ceremony, including sexual ones. Not the years when I was 'in my prime,' and the kids acted as a very efficient deterrent to many a well-planned rendezvous."

She notes that in the older-but-wiser stage, "The ground of understanding, affection, and experience has been tilled. The hormones are still pumping pretty good, and Cupid finds he has a couple of pros to work with."

But like the initial phase of relationships, the excitement of the older-but-wiser stage often fades. It can be a complicated season, as couples reconnect and sometimes discover they've grown apart in certain ways. Family crises seem to pop up every week, and aging bodies don't always cooperate. Your younger sister may want to go on a girls' cruise and swim with the dolphins, while your idea of fun is reading a good book on the beach. Perhaps your parents are becoming less compliant and more demanding as they age, or your children aren't living up to your expectations. Or maybe your concept of how to be a wonderful, concerned grandparent doesn't gel with your daughter-in-law's opinions about your involvement in her family's lives.

In any relationship and in any stage, we need to give each other understanding, remain patient with life's changes, and continue to be creative. It may take some time, but we *will* get our sea legs, if we stay loyal, positive, and focused on God and each other.

With loved ones, we need to learn to keep short accounts, as we discussed in the last chapter, and to not become embroiled in anger and grievances with one another. When we do, and an argument stretches into days—maybe even weeks—it poisons the tone of our relationships and surroundings. Satan loves to shove a wedge of bitterness and unforgivingness between people. Those two toxic emotions grow rapidly, and prevent us from seeing things from a godly perspective. Before long, we're holding grudges and creating lists of grievances. Not a pretty sight.

In fact, Satan loves to use anything to create a wall between Christian parents and children, brothers and sisters, cousins and in-laws, friends, co-workers, and co-worshippers. We must continually be on our guard against his wicked schemes. Ephesians 6:10–13 says, "Finally, be strong in the

Lord and in his mighty power. Put on the full armor of God so that you can take your stand against the devil's schemes. For our struggle is not against flesh and blood, but against the rulers, against the authorities, against the powers of this dark world and against the spiritual forces of evil in the heavenly realms. Therefore put on the full armor of God, so that when the day of evil comes, you may be able to stand your ground, and after you have done everything, to stand" (NIV).

Make no mistake, ladies: We are in a battlefield. The devil wants to destroy our godly relationships. So each day, we must pray against his workings and keep God's truth in the forefront of our minds and lives. We must stand firm—if not for ourselves, then for our friends, spouses, siblings, children, and parents. How do we do that? By staying "girded up" with scripture, godly fellowship, and time alone with the Lord.

There's only been one perfect relationship, and that was the pairing of Adam and Eve with God when the Creator walked with His children in the Garden of Eden. Then that wily serpent, Satan, came along, deceived Eve—who disobeyed God, as did Adam—and sin entered the picture. The world has been full of dysfunctional families and misguided friendships ever since.

A counselor once told me, "If you were the perfect parent, your kids wouldn't need God." What relief! I don't have to perfect, because God is.

Still, God longs for us to have healing and an abundant

life here on earth, and not just in heaven (where all our relationships will be like the one God, Adam, and Eve shared in the Garden). In John 10:10, Jesus says, "'A thief is only there to steal and kill and destroy. I came so they can have real and eternal life, more and better life than they ever dreamed of'" (MSG).

Just as he deceived Eve by convincing her to sin (and then enticing Adam to imitate her), Satan has had a hand in all our messed-up relationships ever since. He loves to steal our joy and kill our hope. He gleefully watches as person after person is destroyed by misunderstandings, betrayals, money worries, unforgivingness, bitterness, and dysfunction.

BALLAST

So how can we have a better life than we've ever dreamed of? It's not easy. Just ask Randi.

Like many older adults, Randi and her husband found that their empty nest wasn't empty for long. Her daughter moved out of their home three separate times. The last time she moved back, she came with her husband and toddler in tow. Randi says, "They had both legal problems and difficulty finding jobs. They moved in on an emergency basis and were supposed to stay for 'a couple of months,' but it stretched to nearly a year."

Randi says they should have been more strategic about coming up with an exit plan for their daughter and her family: "Without clear communication about expectations *before* they moved in, we set ourselves up to be used (and resented) by my daughter. It nearly destroyed our relationship."

Now, several years later, the relationship is significantly improved. Randi says gratefully, "My daughter is in a much better place with God, and we continue to patiently rebuild what has been damaged. . .by both of us."

Sandra, another woman in the sandwich generation, sees her mom making similar mistakes with her brother. Sandra's mother, who is almost eighty-eight, suffers from nervousness, anxiety, fear, confusion, sleepwalking/-talking. . .all stemming from a restless, fearful spirit. Sandra says, "She cannot find comfort in her Christian faith because to acknowledge Jesus as Savior means to go against my brother, who has become a Buddhist. Instead she has embraced a universal-god theory that all beliefs lead to a God who would never send anybody to hell."

Sandra longs for her mom to speak the truth to her brother. She believes that for those of us with children, it sometimes becomes necessary to confront them with an uncomfortable truth, whether that's about faith, sexuality, or any number of issues. "We as parents have to be strong enough to say, 'If I speak truth to this child, I may lose them for my lifetime, but if I don't, I may lose them for eternity.'

From the story of the prodigal son, we see that the father did not follow after the son into a life of sin. The father stayed put, praying and waiting, becoming an anchor to which the son could return when he came to his senses. We should never follow anyone, child or husband into sin. I believe this is the source of my mother's painful, fearful life."

Allison Bottke, a dynamic writer, speaker, and entrepreneur, says there's a big difference between helping and enabling. She notes, "*Helping* is doing something for someone that he is not capable of doing himself. *Enabling* is doing for someone things that he could and should be doing himself. An enabler is a person who recognizes that a negative circumstance is occurring on a regular basis and yet continues to enable the person with the problem to persist with his detrimental behaviors. Simply, enabling creates an atmosphere in which our adult children can comfortably continue with their unacceptable behavior."[6]

So the first step to finding abundant life in the midst of friend and family relationships is to *stop enabling*. We cannot make other people change. Only they can make the choices (including yielding to God) that lead to freedom. And we must realize this, or we'll spend our lives miserable, trying to "make" things happen.

The second step to finding that "best life" that Jesus talks about in John 10:10 is to *seek His face*. Have you surrendered your painful relationships to Him? Have you given them to

[6] From www.settingboundaries.com/six-steps/. Used with permission.

Him for safekeeping, taking your hands off once and for all? Good. Then trust Him—fully, not just partly—to work them out in His own time and way.

God's Word says, " 'Tomorrow go down against them. . . . You will not need to fight in this battle. Position yourselves, stand still and see the salvation of the LORD, who is with you. . . .' Do not fear or be dismayed" (2 Chronicles 20:16–17 NKJV). So, when you've done all you can, having been honest, confessed your own shortcomings, and set appropriate boundaries, just stand still, leaving the rest to God.

Refuse to participate in unhealthy behavior and guard against feeling hopeless, because that's what Satan wants. Refuse to linger in sadness and frustration. Instead, continue to pray and do the things you can. Confide in those who are wiser than you; receive their guidance, and act on it. And trust God to work, even when you can't see His hand, for the battle is His.

Consider Barbara, a woman who is trusting God with her aging mother's future. They have a wonderful relationship. But recently, she admitted her ninety-year-old mom to a nursing home in their small Texas town. And for Barbara, it was painful.

Barbara's mom lived alone—first in her home, then in an assisted living facility—for twenty-four years after her husband died, so the transition into a new place where she would share a small space with a roommate was a big one.

Barbara worried that her mom would be unhappy and upset, but her mom told her that nursing homes did not scare her.

When Barbara wheeled her into the center's dining room, her mom recognized a couple of women and they got reacquainted. Barbara says, "As I looked at the wheelchair-bound women chatting, what impressed me most was the courage they all possessed. I assume they are all cognizant of the probability of this home being their last residence on earth. But they do not appear to be frightened."

Courage. That's what the third—and perhaps most important—step in finding abundant life within our relationships demands. This step is *to say the hard things*, whether those are words of love, chastisement, or a combination of both. Sometimes we need to tell a child she's not allowed to live with us anymore; other times, we may have to tell a parent that we need to place him in a nursing or assisted living facility; or be honest with a friend or relative if she is coming on too strong with advice or is too interfering in our lives. Remember, God is with us in the midst of our difficulties. He can give us the strength to say the achingly difficult stuff.

Sometimes those words are ones of love and encouragement. If you grew up in a nonaffectionate family or in a dysfunctional atmosphere, saying "I love you" or "I appreciate all you've done for me" may be the hardest thing of all. But I encourage you to pray for the strength to give words of love to those who need them. As we've mentioned before, life is short, and we have no guarantee of more time with those we love.

A few years ago, for Father's Day, Carol gave her dad a letter filled with the memories she had of him. She also made copies for her kids—his grandkids.

She wrote, "Time has passed all too quickly and I have children of my own. Each day I realize how hard and just how important being a parent really is. In the process I am learning what wonderful parents I had. I love him as only a 'little girl' can love her daddy. HAPPY FATHER'S DAY 1983, DADDY!"

Carol said the hard things, before it was too late.

There's a biblical mother-in-law and daughter-in-law duo, Naomi and Ruth, who also mutually admired each other. They epitomize this third step. Naomi and Ruth came from different places and had little in common, yet their love for each other overcame their dissimilarities. When Naomi's and Ruth's husbands died, Naomi urged her daughter-in-law Ruth to leave her and go back to her own people. But Ruth famously replied, "Don't urge me to leave you or to turn back from you. Where you go I will go, and where you stay I will stay. Your people will be my people and your God my God. Where you die I will die, and there I will be buried. May the LORD deal with me, be it ever so severely, if anything but death separates you and me" (Ruth 1:16–17 NIV).

Everyone would have understood if Ruth had made a different decision. But Ruth was utterly committed to her "mother-in-love," and she steadfastly refused to leave Naomi alone. Instead, Ruth declared her bond with Naomi unbreakable and wouldn't budge. Ruth said the hard thing. And history was changed forever because of it.

Ruth's promise to Naomi has lasted thousands of years and is still spoken during modern wedding ceremonies. Boaz, a kinsman of Ruth and Naomi, heard of Ruth's selflessness and took her as his wife. Eventually, Boaz and Ruth had a son, who was in the line of David and, ultimately, the Son of God.

It's true! Naomi's grandson, Obed, was an ancestor to Jesus! God's miraculous plan overcame all sorts of hurt and grief. And He can do the same for us.

SETTING A COURSE

Like Ruth, we must speak the hard things. We must declare our unwavering love for our family members (even the ones we can't stand!) and friends, and then move out of the way and let God work. We can give our friends, children, parents, siblings, cousins, and other relatives our fervent compassion even when we disagree with them.

Sometimes, saying that we love someone unconditionally is the hardest thing to do, especially when she's acting as if she hates us—and perhaps, everything we stand for. But our model is God, who never fails to love us, even when we sin.

Loving people without limits doesn't mean we approve of their behavior or lifestyle—it just means that we're there for them, with a heart full of love, no matter how they act. (Isn't this how God responds to us, His dear children?) And if or when the individuals concerned decide to make the right choices and seek our and God's forgiveness, we must welcome them back with open arms.

God can redeem any situation, any person—no matter how horrible the past.

Who have you given up on? Who have you written off, thinking he's no good and will never change? Is it a child, a parent, a relative? Do you wish she would just go away and leave you alone—forever? Is the person wreaking havoc in your life, and you're tired of it?

Don't give up. God hasn't written you off, and He's not finished with your difficult person, either. So quit enabling—but keep praying. Seek His face, and give up worrying. Say the hard things—and never, ever stop hoping.

You never know what God will do. . .even—especially—in you.

☾ SMOOTH SAILING

No matter what relationship stage we are in with our loved ones, we can control only one thing: our own behavior. Consider that as you navigate the often-stormy waters of relationships with imperfect people. (And remember, you make lots of mistakes, too!) Vow to be forgiving, because Jesus set the ultimate example when He forgave those who killed Him. Most of all, lean on the Lord as you sail into the winds of change—for those winds affect friendships, family members, and marriages, too. Trust Him to anchor your heart in the truth, and to not lead you astray. As others make their choices—good or bad—give them to the Lord in prayer, instead of fretting about their decisions. And give thanks for the low-maintenance, positive, and encouraging people God has put in your life. They're the sails that help your craft stay upright when you face the hazards that aging brings. Here's some truth to chew on as you ponder your position with people:

- *Don't lose your grip on Love and Loyalty. Tie them around your neck; carve their initials on your heart. Earn a reputation for living well in God's eyes and the eyes of the people.*
  Proverbs 3:3 msg

- *I've commanded you to be strong and brave. Don't ever be afraid or discouraged! I am the Lord your God, and I will be there to help you wherever you go.*
  Joshua 1:9 cev

- *" 'Honor your father and mother; and love your neighbor as you love yourself.' "*
  Matthew 19:19 ncv

- *Let your unfailing love surround us, Lord, for our hope is in you alone.*
  Psalm 33:22 nlt

- *"If you obey my commands, you will remain in my love, just as I have obeyed my Father's commands and remain in his love."*
  John 15:10 niv

Chapter 5

Keep the Faith

My memory's not as sharp as it used to be.
Also, my memory's not as sharp as it used to be.
UNKNOWN

◯ THE DRIFT

"*Where* is my Sunday paper?" demanded an irate customer when she called the newspaper office.

"Ma'am," said an employee, "Today is Saturday. The Sunday paper is not delivered until tomorrow. . .on Sunday."

There was a long pause on the other end of the line. Then the woman said, "So that's why no one was at church today!"

Can you relate? As we get older, our minds don't always work the way we'd like them to. We walk in a room and forget why we're there. We live by lists and find that even the simplest things slip our mind.

Memory loss is one of the challenges of aging, for sure—but there are things we can do to help us from becoming too forgetful. Consider these ideas:

- *Try taking ginkgo biloba or vitamin E.* In one study, of those taking ginkgo, 27 percent maintained cognitive functioning and memory, while 86 percent of the placebo group lost functioning. Be careful, though—ginkgo increases aspirin's blood-thinning effects.
- *Drink coffee.* Certain studies suggest that two strong cups a day can help ward off dementia and Alzheimer's. (Not a bad reason to keep drinking your daily cup of joe!)
- *Keep your mind active.* Try sudoku, do crossword puzzles, play Scrabble, and read the paper. Write your

memoirs, one paragraph at a time. Discuss politics, and buy books of brain teasers to work through.
- *Reduce stress as much as possible.* When you're anxious, your brain is preoccupied and isn't able to handle its daily load as well.
- *Eat well.* Foods rich in antioxidants (dark berries, dark chocolate—yes, chocolate!—and broccoli) or omega 3 (olive oil, nuts, fish) give your brain extra nutrients that help it to function better. Also, a diet full of plants and vegetables seems to help prevent many diseases and can't hurt your memory, either!
- *Take your pills.* Don't neglect your medicine for conditions like high cholesterol or high blood pressure, since those illnesses can negatively affect your mind. (Also, get those numbers checked regularly, because left untreated, both high cholesterol and high blood pressure can lead to memory loss.)
- *Get together with friends often.*
- *Be on the lookout for signs of depression* (more about this later in the chapter). Older adults who are depressed are at risk for becoming confused and forgetful.
- *Avoid head injuries if at all possible*—wear safety equipment when you participate in sports, and make your home safer to avoid falls.
- *Don't overindulge in alcohol.*
- *Get enough sleep.*[7]

---

[7] These tips gleaned from www.howtodothings.com/health-and-fitness/a1938-how-to-prevent-memory-loss.html.

That last point might pose a problem, if you're like many maturing women. Insomnia can hit around the mid-century mark, or sometimes earlier—during perimenopause. Sandy says, "I will be forty-nine in October. I have just started getting hot flashes but still have my cycle, although it has become irregular. When I don't get a good night's sleep, too often the next day I end up falling asleep during the six o'clock news. That causes a problem for that night's sleep, and then I get into a cycle I have to work to break."

Sandy's discovered that the more sugar she eats, the more difficult sleeping is. She's also discovered that she can't have caffeine after noon, and notes that regular exercise helps her sleep better.

Heather, Rebekah, and Lisa have restless legs syndrome. Heather swears by a hot bath before bed, while Rebekah stretches and takes Advil before retiring for the night. Lisa takes an anti-inflammatory every night. She says, "Persistent insomnia is a sign to me that I have too many things going on in my life. I usually find if I can 'get rid' of some of the busyness in my life, I am able to get some sleep."

Tamma says the prescription Lunesta is her "best friend" to help her sleep.

LaBrenda tries to take a walk about one to two hours before she goes to bed: "Not anything strenuous, just an easy pace. And all the lights in my house go out except a lamp thirty minutes before bedtime."

LaBrenda has a friend who puts a notebook and pen beside her bed, so if she wakes up and starts thinking about all she needs to do, she writes it down. She's then able to go back to sleep.

Debra drinks a glass of milk before bed, which helps her calm down and not toss and turn.

Melanie suffers from sleep apnea, and has to wear a mask that delivers air pressure via a continuous positive airway pressure (CPAP) machine. It took a trip to a sleep clinic to get diagnosed, and the contraption took some getting used to, but the CPAP has helped her to sleep through the night—for the first time in years.

If you're suffering from insomnia and have tried all these things and more, with no relief, don't despair. There is hope! Most doctors agree on these steps to ensure a better night's sleep:

- *Create a sleep routine.* Don't vary it unless you have to.
- *Drink hot chamomile tea and try other herbal remedies.* Kava, valerian, and other herbs may help some women sleep better. Melatonin, a synthetic reproduction of a hormone that occurs naturally in our bodies, works for many people.[8]
- *Keep your television, cell phone, and iPod out of the bedroom.*
- *Use a white-noise machine or fan to drown out crickets, dogs, traffic, or other annoying noises.*

---

[8] See www.smartbomb.com/sleepandrelt.html for more information.

- *If you're married and your husband snores, try to get him to a doctor or sleep clinic.* If he won't go and nothing over the counter works, sleep in the guest room or on the couch. Your rest is superimportant—and you can still use the bedroom for lovemaking.

Finally, if you're really desperate, you may need to talk to your doctor about one of the prescription sleep medications on the market. Most of them are non–habit-forming, and the best of them don't make you groggy the next day.

Besides memory lapses and sleep difficulties, another challenge for many aging women is their low libido. In fact, one of my friends (who shall remain anonymous) sent me her two cents about sex:

You know you are a married mom of four when...

...foreplay is hearing your hubby click the lock on the bedroom door.

...you fake sleep to avoid sex not because you are tired, but because you are having an "I'm feeling fat" sort of day.

...you go into Victoria's Secret because your husband begged you to buy a thong to surprise him, and you leave empty-handed because they were all way too small.

...you wish they made sexy looking Spanx (i.e.,

slimming intimate apparel).

. . .romance is getting the kids to bed early so you can fall asleep on the couch with your hubby while watching *American Idol* by candlelight.

Do you feel that way? Does the thought of sexual intimacy just make you tired? If so, there are probably a number of reasons why you'd rather get a root canal than make love.

As we get older, our hormone levels drop, and that alone can cause huge changes in our desire. Also, women who suffer from hypothyroidism or other physical conditions like fibromyalgia have special issues with regard to sex—low energy, aching bodies, etc. Those who've undergone chemo and surgery (especially a mastectomy) have their own challenges.

And then there's the stress of getting older—changing relationships, priorities, and finances. Marriages can splinter and crack when kids leave, and sex might fall by the wayside. Or aging parents may take all our time and energy.

Whatever the reasons behind a low sex drive, realize that you can have a fulfilling sex life as an older adult. God created us as sexual beings, and He's given us myriad resources to help us in having a healthy life (spirit, soul, and body). Here are a few ideas to help you in that area:

- *See a hormone specialist and get your levels checked.*

Stress and aging affect progesterone, estrogen, and testosterone—which all affect libido. Natural replacements are one solution, and they don't have the side effects that older synthetic hormones do.
- *Talk to a counselor.* Sometimes, issues from our past contribute to shame and fear in the area of sex.
- *Keep the communication lines open with your husband, and tell him you want to work on things.* Just knowing you care will go a long way. Also, tell him your needs and wants, even if you feel "funny" talking about it.
- *Eat healthy and exercise.* It helps every area of our lives when we take care of the body God's given us. Consider this: "Very few of us recognize the connection between nutrition and libido. A lifetime of nutritional deficiencies creates the preconditions for hormonal imbalance. Chronic dieting has a terrible impact on your energy and self-image, and therefore on your sex drive. Low-fat diets are a special problem, because your body needs lipids to make its hormones, including the testosterone needed for sexual response." [9]
- *Don't give up!* You can find the answer, and feel better.

With commitment, communication, and godly concern for each other, couples can work through these problems.

---

[9] Holmes, Marcy, NP, and Dixie Mills, MD, *Low Sex Drive in Women: Causes and Solutions,* www.womentowomen.com/sexualityandfertility/sexaftermenopause.aspx.

What if you can't work through your marriage problems, sexual or otherwise? Davina says, "I was married for eleven years. He was a womanizer and ran around on me, so we divorced, and then I rebounded and married again."

Davina's second marriage lasted for twenty-three years, but it was very rocky. She finally divorced her second husband and has now been single for three and a half years.

She says, "I've found support in my family with my sister. I also have two boys who are there for me if I need them. It's been tough, but I got through it with a Christian counselor and the grace of God. I'm still taking it a day at a time."

She worries about finances, and since she also survived breast cancer and underwent a bilateral mastectomy in 2002, she says honestly, "I wonder how that will affect my finding someone to share the rest of my life with."

But she notes, "I've definitely gotten closer to the Lord. I've gotten time to spend with God, reflect, and get to know myself."

If you're in the same boat as Davina, know that you've got good company. With many women living longer than men, the numbers of women living alone doubled between 1970 and 1998, from 7.3 million to 15.3 million. The 2000 U.S. Census Report stated that half of the women living alone were elderly—which means that 41 percent of all elderly women lived by themselves. That's a huge number!

And many divorced, widowed, or never-married women

have the opposite of low libido—lots of desire for a physical connection, but no partner. If you're in that boat, find someone trustworthy to talk to about it, and lean into God. He created you and approves of you. He can handle your frustration and loneliness. Nothing is a surprise to Him, and nothing is too difficult for Him, either.

Remember that even though our stations in life change, God's Word doesn't. And neither do His laws. God wants us to honor Him with our body, and that includes saving sex for marriage. Don't give yourself, body and soul, to someone for the sake of temporary companionship. God can give you strength to stand by your convictions and not make the wrong choices when your desire threatens to overwhelm your commitment to purity.

Sometimes, the loneliness inherent in living alone (compounded by the grief of losing someone you love to death or divorce, or the frustration of never marrying, for those who'd like to find a spouse) can lead to depression.

My family tree is full of people who've suffered from depression. One of those is my mother, Susie Ratliff. She says, "I have found God to be an all-loving, caring, and compassionate Savior, but He (in my case) has forced me to walk some very long and difficult roads to find Him my closest friend."

Mom is an only child who had a "distant-but-pleasant" relationship with her folks. She never knew what it was to have a daily walk with God until she met her future husband—my dad. Dad showed Mom what it meant to be a Christian.

Early in their marriage, she sank into a deep depression. And she says, "Although I was never diagnosed with a nervous breakdown, I believe I had one. There was no money for doctors or therapy, and depression was not discussed openly in the l960s. It was a mental illness and was swept under the rug. Every moment for me dragged on like an hour. I couldn't concentrate on anything, worried about everything, and feared I might have a horrible illness. And I did—depression."

The scripture God gave her through that rough time was James l:2–6: "Consider it all joy, my brethren, when you encounter various trials, knowing that the testing of your faith produces endurance. And let endurance have its perfect result, so that you may be perfect and complete, lacking in nothing. But if any of you lacks wisdom, let him ask of God, who gives to all generously and without reproach, and it will be given to him. But he must ask in faith without any doubting, for the one who doubts is like the surf of the sea, driven and tossed by the wind" (NASB).

With the Lord's help, that scripture, and a long-needed change in her work atmosphere, Mom began to pull out of a deep pit of despair. She says, "God was merciful and my health, both physical and mental, slowly began improving."

Like Mom, I've had my share of depression. It's something I wouldn't wish on my worst enemy. Looking back, I can remember times as a teen where I was probably depressed and not just "moody." But my first bout of clinical depression was brought on by a series of losses, including an early miscarriage, moving, and financial worries.

Maybe you've been there. On the outside, you keep everything together. You couldn't suffer from depression, could you? What would people say?

You feel ashamed. Mostly, because you feel God has abandoned you, and you don't know where to turn. Maybe you're sleeping much of the time. Perhaps you suffer from a racing heart and shortness of breath. Or your appetite is gone, and you have no energy. You feel despair. And you see no way out.

When I was going under, I went to a Christian counseling clinic. For months, for an hour once a week, I sat with a lovely woman and poured out my story. I don't remember much of the advice she gave me, but I know she listened. She also recommended I work through the book *Search for Significance.*

Those weeks literally changed my life by teaching me to replace the lies I had believed (I have to be perfect; God can't love me; I'm only significant when I'm accomplishing things) with the truth from His word (God loves me unconditionally; He's the only perfect one; and I don't have to do a thing to be loved by Him).

My counselor also helped me find other tools to keep the disease at bay. I now make time to take my medications, read and meditate on scripture, connect deeply with friends and family members, exercise, and reach out to others who are hurting. There's nothing like seeing others who are worse off than ourselves to put things in perspective!

Do you have trouble laughing or crying, or do you hardly ever experience great joy? Has a season of appropriate grief gone on for much longer than you expected? You might just be depressed. You could be stuck under a "cloud of gray." Depression can manifest itself in a variety of ways. Some depressed people suffer from insomnia, and others want to sleep constantly. Many find themselves in a state of confusion or forgetfulness. Others get angry and can't seem to find joy in even little things that used to make them happy.

If you think you're depressed, please don't let Satan convince you that you're a bad person or that you'll never recover. There is freedom on the other side! Please don't suffer in silence! And you don't have to "suck it up" and "pull yourself up by your bootstraps." You just need help.

Depression isn't a sin or a weakness. It's an illness. Some of the Bible's most celebrated individuals experienced times of emotional darkness and doubt—including King David, Moses, Job, Jonah, and Elijah. Jesus Himself thought God had abandoned Him on the cross. So you're not crazy, you're not alone, and you're not just "weak."

When Elijah was depressed, he had just had a huge victory against Queen Jezebel. He came off the mountaintop of success and crashed—hard. He even told God he wanted to die. So God sent an angel to minister to Elijah. The angel fed Elijah, told him to get some rest, and encouraged his soul. Good food, supportive friends (the greatest of which is Jesus!), and rest—all are still great ways to take care of yourself when you feel hopeless and exhausted.

Do you believe you're suffering from depression? Here are a few action steps I urge you to take:

- *Admit you need help.* Ask a doctor and/or counselor to guide you in finding the right combination of rest, medicine, and counseling so you can get—and stay—well.
- *Set small daily goals.* If you can, make yourself take a shower, get dressed, and get out of the house. Even though it's hard, it will help you.
- *Exercise.* Exercise increases a feeling of well-being because it releases endorphins. Even if you just walk around the block, the sunshine can help you feel better.
- *Surround yourself with positive people.* (But be careful about Pollyannas—who don't think depression is an illness and believe it's all in your mind.) Optimism is contagious; so is pessimism.
- *Find clean, silly movies and television shows to watch, as well as books to read*—laughter releases the same kind of mood-enhancing chemicals as exercise does.

- *Share your struggle with people who will be understanding.* Be selective, and pick the people who have been there or who know you well and won't judge you. Sharing your feelings will keep you from bottling things up and making the depression worse.

What if it's not you, but someone you love who's depressed? That situation brings its own struggles. Maybe you feel at a loss as to what to say and do. You might feel confused, because your loved one wants to be alone—and you don't know if that's good or bad for him or her. Perhaps you feel isolated, because you don't know anyone who's in your situation.

Don't despair—please! There are support groups for people just like you. You can find one in your area, or on the Internet. Those who are going through the same thing will be a lifeline and sanity saver for you.

If you're wondering what steps to take to help your depressed friend or family member, here are some ways to aid (and not add to the despair of) your loved one:

- *Encourage them to get help from a doctor and/or counselor.* Some depressions are chemically based and need medical intervention.
- *Listen to them and ask them what (if anything) they need from you.* Then try to give them space and time to get better.
- *Pray for them* (and with them, if they feel comfortable with it).

- *If you don't live with the depressed loved one, call and check on them as much as you can, and offer to help with tasks that are overwhelming* (paying bills, getting groceries, caring for grandchildren, etc.).
- *Be patient*—recovery can take a long time. Know that it's a marathon and not a sprint.
- *Don't judge or criticize.* If you feel frustrated, try to share that without condemning them. They aren't trying to frazzle you or cause you grief, and they may not be very responsive to your caring overtures. Don't take it personally.
- *Don't tell them to "just snap out of it" or "just trust the Lord."* You may get angry at their lack of initiative or emotional involvement with you, but try to stay calm as you share your feelings with them.
- *Don't just quote Bible verses at them.* If anything, write an encouraging note with some scripture in it—but try not to preach to them. If they are Christian, they believe in God and in scripture, but it's in their head and isn't getting through to their heart right now.
- *Don't try to "fix it."*

My family and I are proof that God can and does heal depression. My relationships with my mother and my husband are deeper and stronger now, because of what we've been through. And God has given me empathy, as well as a ministry to others who are hurting. I've heard it said, "Your biggest test will become your testimony," and that's been true for us, praise God!

Perhaps you're not depressed, but you still feel frustrated by the season you're in. Maybe the life you longed for hasn't appeared yet, and you wonder if God has gone missing. Are your prayers for peace, a good marriage, finding your one true love, or just relief from hot flashes going unanswered?

BALLAST

Whether you're aching for sleep or for Prince Charming, life can be hard. We've all waited—or are presently waiting—on a dream to be fulfilled. Some women long for a mate, while others pine for a dream job.

What do we do when the job doesn't come through, the marriage doesn't get better, or our prayers for a spouse seem to fall on deaf ears? Do we get bitter, question our faith? After all, the "prosperity theology" many current evangelical leaders spout—i.e., "God wants us to be happy, so He'll give us good things"—doesn't have room for poverty, sickness, or unanswered prayers (unless it's due to sin).

That kind of theology also doesn't have room for sacrifice and suffering—so it leaves out about half the Bible. It leaves out the cross. And if you leave out the cross, the gospel isn't the gospel.

Though I do believe that God loves us and blesses His children, the totality of scripture instead points toward the fact that God wants us to be holy, and although He does love to bless His children, His gifts do not necessarily come when we'd expect them.

Sometimes, we obey God's call and find that life gets harder, not easier. What do we do when that happens? Do we try to cash in our refund?

At times, we may want to turn our back on the whole "faith" thing. It's not always a quick fix. And we may not be very patient. . .which is probably why God is still working on us! And yet we find that we can't give God up. Okay—scratch that. The truth is, He won't give up on us.

Look at Job. When Satan asked God to sift the man like wheat, God agreed—as long as Satan would spare Job's life. The "why" of that interchange escapes me. God obviously loved Job, but He allowed Satan to take everything—children, health, business, reputation—from His faithful servant.

And Job was faithful to the nth degree. His friends urged him to repent, because they believed Job's losses were the result of sin, and even his wife encouraged him to curse God and die. But Job stood firm, because he knew he was innocent. Still, Job was human—so he questioned God.

But instead of addressing the "why" of the situation, God answered "out of the storm" (Job 38:1 NIV) and asked

Job tons of questions. He pointed to all the mysterious and miraculous ways of nature, saying, "Look, Job, you'll never understand My ways. Just know this: I'm perfect, I'm here, and I will never leave you."

And Job repented—not of his sin, but of his narrow worldview. In Job 42:2–5, he replied to the Lord: "I know that you can do all things; no plan of yours can be thwarted. You asked, 'Who is this that obscures my counsel without knowledge?' Surely I spoke of things I did not understand, things too wonderful for me to know. You said, 'Listen now, and I will speak; I will question you, and you shall answer me.' My ears had heard of you but now my eyes have seen you" (NIV).

The book of Job is in the Bible not to give us all the answers to life's suffering, but to show us that although loss is a guarantee, so is God's presence. Our worldview is so narrow. Our perspective is skewed by our past, our culture, and our limited vision. All we can see is what's happening to us. . .not the things happening around the world or situations that will unfold generations from now, and certainly not the actions taking place in the spiritual realm.

In the book of Daniel, an angel came to Daniel after he had been praying fervently for three weeks for God to reveal the meaning of a dream to him. The angel told Daniel: "Sorry—I was busy with a spiritual battle, or I would have been here sooner" (Daniel 10:13, author's paraphrase).

We can't know how our story will unfold, or how it affects all the other stories God is writing. When we feel buffeted by life's winds, may we have the same reaction as Job. When the storm rages and threatens to capsize our craft, I pray we will say with Job, "Okay. I don't get this, but I know You're here. I will trust that You have me in the palm of Your hand, and that will be enough."

If we let Him, our faithful Father will continue to stretch us, push us, and take us to the next level in our faith-walk. It's not always easy, but it's always worth it. And in the midst of the journey, if we have eyes to see, we'll discover we've found treasures in the darkness—lots of them.

God gives us peace and joy in the midst of suffering. He gives us Christian friends and family members who spur us on to love and good deeds. And each day, when we're quiet and watchful enough to see them, we realize once more that He continually gives us eternal (not always material!) blessings at His right hand.

There's nothing wrong with wanting good things from life, but we need to strike a balance between hoping for the future and living in the moment. It's difficult to find that middle ground, but it's also imperative if we're to live with joy in our current circumstances.

The pathway to joy starts when we entrust our cares to Him, believing that He knows best and will give us what we need, when we need it (and not before). Sure, we may have to wait longer than *we* think is necessary for certain dreams to come true. Still, we can rest in God's love for us, knowing that He knows us better than we know ourselves, and He is working out a perfect design for our lives.

Liz says, "One day at the grocery checkout line, I stood on one foot and then the other. My back hurt, my head hurt, and a dirty kitchen and sick husband waited for me at home. With angry thoughts in my heart and hateful words threatening to spew out my mouth at the checker, I scratched my neck and my hand rested on the beautiful cross my husband had given me for Christmas. It was as if my heavenly Father whispered, 'Either take off the cross that shouts "I'm a Christian," or speak healing words.' "

Liz gripped the grocery basket and managed to get out of the store without causing a scene. She says, "By choice, I care for my grown daughter who is somewhat disabled and my husband's health is also deteriorating. So at seventy-two years old, instead of slowing down and being a graceful, sweet old lady, my obligations and responsibilities are increasing. In addition, proper sleep is a joke, rest is impossible, and I felt that my days of sharing the love of Jesus had come to an end. Even if my energy would allow, there was no time left in any of my hectic days to do anything of value for my Lord."

She wanted to remind God that she was tired and that she'd given up a lot in order to be faithful to the changes in her life. "Instead," she says, "while I cleaned up the kitchen, through hot tears, I asked Him to forgive me and to teach me. I'm still tired and life has not gotten easier. But God changed my attitude, and I've found a whole new ministry. As God provides grace, I am amazed how much I smile these days and—no matter how my back aches—I hear myself speak words of encouragement and cheer to clerks, shopkeepers, waiters, strangers on the street. Yes, and even to regular family and friends! Obviously, God thinks I can serve Him even when I'm tired!"

SMOOTH SAILING

When you're struggling with endless nights and dark days like Liz, let God's light be your comfort. Hold on to scripture, your godly friends, and Him. Let Him restore your hope.

Corrie ten Boom once said, "The deepest darkness is outshone by the love of Jesus." He loves you way more than you could ever fathom. Lean on that fact, and trust that He will never leave you or forsake you.

One way to find strength to believe is to meditate on His promises, and praise Him for the prayers He's answered thus far. Write thankful prayers and praises in a journal, and add to it every day. Also, record the following promises in your journal, along with the things you're praying and waiting for. By doing so, you'll be creating a record of God's goodness.

- *It is good that one should be quiet and wait for the saving power of the Lord.*
  LAMENTATIONS 3:26 NLV

- *When you lie down, you will not be afraid; when you lie down, your sleep will be sweet.*
  PROVERBS 3:24 NIV

- *Why are you down in the dumps, dear soul? Why are you crying the blues? Fix my eyes on God—soon I'll be praising again. He puts a smile on my face. He's my God.*
  PSALM 42:5 MSG

- *Indeed, we had the sentence of death within ourselves so that we would not trust in ourselves, but in God who raises the dead; who delivered us from so great a peril of death, and will deliver us, He on whom we have set our hope. And He will yet deliver us.*
  2 CORINTHIANS 1:9–10 NASB

- *Wait patiently for the LORD. Be brave and courageous. Yes, wait patiently for the LORD.*
  PSALM 27:14 NLT

- *I will lie down and sleep in peace, for you alone, O LORD, make me dwell in safety.*
  PSALM 4:8 NIV

Chapter 6

Cultivate Community

Friends are God's way of apologizing to us for our families.
Anonymous

THE DRIFT

Remember Anne from Lucy Maud Montgomery's classic, *Anne of Green Gables*? The spunky redheaded orphan made everything into an adventure and lived with a grand sense of the dramatic. She was also fond of the term "bosom friends."

Bosom friends are blessings from God. Those kinds of buddies laugh with you, cry with you, and pull you up when you're down. As we sail this sea of changes, nothing can encourage us like good girlfriends.

Simply put, friends are good medicine for women's souls—and even for our bodies. University of Iowa's Susan Lutgendorf studied twenty-four women with ovarian cancer and five with benign pelvic masses. The women with healthy friendships had lower levels of a protein that fuels cancerous growth. Pretty amazing stuff!

Research also shows that not staying connected to other people poses similar risks to your health as medical problems like high blood pressure, obesity, and even smoking. Todd Jackson, PhD, authored a 2006 study that found that people who had large social networks also had healthier diet, exercise, and sleep habits. And a 2005 New England study showed that people who had an exercise buddy lost much more weight than those who went the solo route.[10]

Ecclesiastes 4:9–12 says, "Two are better than one,

---

[10] See yourtotalhealth.ivillage.com/friends-with-benefits-friends-keep-you-healthy.html for more information.

because they have a good reward for their labor. For if they fall, one will lift up his companion. But woe to him who is alone when he falls, for he has no one to help him up. Again, if two lie down together, they will keep warm; but how can one be warm alone? Though one may be overpowered by another, two can withstand him. And a threefold cord is not quickly broken" (NKJV).

Speaker Pam Farrell, author of *Fantastic After 40*, writes, "When building a home, 2x4's are hammered together on bearing walls so they can bear more weight. This term is called 'sistering.' " She says we can apply that to our own lives: "When women stand shoulder to shoulder and *sister* one another, we are stronger, and we can make a positive difference." Pam says that life after forty can, indeed, be fantastic, but it can also be quite challenging: "These years are filled with great memories and exciting moments—and a few trying times."

For Pam, life after forty included holding a friend whose husband announced his affair and left the family, sitting beside a friend in chemotherapy, counseling numerous moms of rebellious teens, and praying with moms of prodigal adult children. In addition, she and her husband Bill began experiencing stress-induced health problems, which led Bill to resign from his job as a pastor. In the meantime, her three teenage sons all got hurt in football games (two of them severely), and her brother suffered a heart attack.

Desperate for joy and peace she prayed, "Lord, I want to be the kind of person who can look at whatever life sends her way and find joy in it. Your Word says, 'The joy of the Lord is our strength' (Nehemiah 8:10) and do I ever need strength right now! So I guess joy is the answer."

She began to deliberately choose joy—and she created a support network for women in their midlife years, many who've had all the same stresses she's endured. It's called *Seasoned Sisters* (www.seasonedsisters.com). *Seasoned Sisters* is an organization of women who gather regularly in friendship circles to gain the strength and education needed to face challenges in this season of their lives. They deliberately choose joy, laugh, learn, pray, and serve together.

Says Pam: "*Seasoned Sisters* is my thank-you to all those precious friends who walked beside me in our midlife transition. It's also my thank-you to God for carrying us through to a strong place and giving me a life to look forward to—no matter what circumstances hit."

◯ BALLAST

As we get older, friends become more important (or they should). Rich relationships are one of God's best gifts to us. As we deal with the inevitable changes our advancing years bring, friends can lift our head, lighten our load, and laugh with us.

Do you have a support network? Are there people in your life with whom you can share your sorrows, struggles, and even shame? Maybe you are dealing with a specific issue (such as setting boundaries with adult children, going through a divorce, or having job difficulties) and need to find a group that will surround you with prayer, advice, and empathy. Perhaps you need a group to walk you through a terrible illness or grief stemming from tragedy. Whatever your need, there's a group for you. Reach out—don't suffer alone. Like-minded friends can lift not only our heads but also our hands and heart.

Moses had those kinds of friends. In Exodus, the Amalekites, enemies of the children of Israel, came and attacked the Israelites. So Moses told Joshua to choose some of their men and "go out to fight the Amalekites. Tomorrow I will stand on top of the hill with the staff of God in my hands" (Exodus 17:9 NIV).

The Bible says, "So Joshua fought the Amalekites as Moses had ordered, and Moses, Aaron and Hur went to the top of the hill. As long as Moses held up his hands, the

Israelites were winning, but whenever he lowered his hands, the Amalekites were winning. When Moses' hands grew tired, they took a stone and put it under him and he sat on it. Aaron and Hur held his hands up—one on one side, one on the other—so that his hands remained steady till sunset. So Joshua overcame the Amalekite army with the sword" (Exodus 17:10–13 NIV).

Aaron and Hur helped Moses in a time of battle by supporting him and loaning him their strength. That's what true friends will do. When we're up against the wall with stress breathing down our necks, friends will call us, take us to a chick flick, and laugh with us. They'll pray for and with us. They'll visit us in the hospital, take care of our pets, feed our husbands (by delivering home-cooked meals), and send flowers. And they'll make sure we have plenty of chocolate.

Just what kinds of friends does a girl's heart good? Here are several:

Praying friend/accountability partner.

If you have friends you can pray with, you're blessed. If not, ask God for friends who have the same desire for accountability, support, and vulnerability as you do. We need more-than-surface friends. We need girlfriends who will cry with us when we're sad, laugh with us when we're happy, and tell us when we need to get a grip. And though it may take some time, God will answer your prayer.

All-in-the-family friend.

After her mother died, Sue found a new friend in her mom's sister, Shelley. Though Shelley has now passed away, Sue says, "Our relationship grew closer after Mother died, because we both missed her. Shelley was not a substitute mom, but we loved each other, and we helped each other through our grief by sharing past memories and building new ones."

Ruth and Naomi were all-in-the-family friends. Allow me a little creative license as I imagine what Naomi might say to us about her daughter-in-law:

> *I loved Ruth from the first moment I met her. There was just something about her. She had a quiet grace, a fervent faith, and a charming way that put people at ease. We used to share stories and jokes as we cooked meals for our husbands. I would tell Ruth stories about my homeland, and she would comfort me in my homesickness. My country of Israel was suffering from a famine, and I knew we had left for good reasons, but I sorely missed my home, friends, and town.*
>
> *Ruth understood. She would regale me with stories about her husband (my son), and she would make me laugh when tears threatened. Although we were very different, she was like a daughter to me. My other daughter-in-law, Orpah, was special to me, too, but she and I didn't have the connection that Ruth and I shared.*

Too soon, life dealt us a horrible blow, and suddenly the three of us had the label widow in common.

You wouldn't believe the amount of tears that flowed as we discussed our future as single women. We didn't have very many options. . .and I was full of fear and anger. I felt angry at God—and though Ruth was grieving as only a newly widowed wife can, she held on to me. I longed for my home, but I'd been gone for ten years. I couldn't decide what to do, and my prayers seemed to bounce off the ceiling.

Finally, I decided to make the long journey back to my hometown alone. I insisted that my daughters-in-law return to their own lands, where they would be more likely to find husbands. Ruth wouldn't hear of it, though. The silly girl was determined to follow me wherever I went. And I loved her even more for it. Together, we faced the crowds who gathered as we returned to Bethlehem. Together, we told my friends and families about the death of our husbands back in Moab.

Though my name means "pleasant," I wouldn't let my people call me that. I wanted them to call me Mara, which means "bitter." I told them: "God has left me with nothing."

But God in His goodness proved me wrong. He gave me Ruth, who would eventually give me a grandson. And over time, He gave me back my joy.

The next kind of necessary confidante is a:

Puzzle-piece friend.

When you plan a getaway together, your puzzle-piece friend yearns to go parasailing—while your idea of bliss is relaxing by the pool with a magazine. Why not join her in her adventurous lifestyle for a bit? It just might do you some good! Sometimes we need to get out of our comfort zones for a little while. This type of friend fills in your gaps. Author Laurie Copeland says, "I spent many years making friends with people just like me. But my best relationships have been with people who were my polar opposite. Like the character Rocky Balboa said, 'We each got our gaps. But together, we ain't got no gaps!' We may rub each other wrong at times, but if we have an open mind to change, we become better people because of our differences."

Passion-sharing friend.

On the other hand, it's great to have friends who share your passions. When we first moved to our current town, I was delighted to find that a fellow mom-writer lived just a few doors down. Megan and I had attended Baylor University together in the late '80s–early '90s and had both studied for a degree in English/professional writing. We had merely been acquaintances there, but since I moved, she's reached out to me and we've become dear friends. We attend a local writers' group together, go on weekly walks, and regularly call and e-mail each other to share our frustrations and joys about motherhood, marriage, and life.

I'm really thankful for Megan. Another kind of encourager is a:

Wise-owl friend.

Sometimes called a *mentor*, this type of friend comes alongside you to support you in your relationship to God and give you exhortation in areas in which you're not comfortable. Mentors can also lead us into a more satisfying career, help us make savvy financial and family decisions, and steer us toward value-driven priorities. My boss's wife has a passion for mentoring, and along with several other moms, she's started a moms' book club. The members meet twice a month to discuss literature that inspires godly mothering—whether it's a book on gratitude, the tone of the home, or discipline.

In a letter to potential group members, the older ladies wrote, "When we were younger women, older women invested in us. We would like to share ideas—about creating an intentional atmosphere/culture within our homes as we serve in our roles as wife, mother, and homemaker. We view it as an opportunity for all of us to discuss our common purpose and to build Christian community." They ended the letter with this passage from Titus 2:3–5: "Older women likewise are to be reverent in their behavior, not malicious gossips nor enslaved to much wine, teaching what is good, so that they may encourage the young women to love their husbands, to love their children, to be sensible, pure, workers at home, kind, being subject to their own husbands, so that the word of God will not be dishonored" (NASB).

It's wonderful that these older, wiser women are taking some younger chicks under their wings. Now, what about you? If you've had life experience of any kind, you can be a mentor, too. Don't be afraid—instead, ask God for ideas about areas in which you could lend your expertise. Inquire at a local Christian Women Job Corps—an organization that always needs godly women to guide younger ladies who are trying to better their lives through education, Bible study, and job placement services.

If you've experienced divorce, singleness, or widowhood, younger women in those situations need a cheerleader. Often, they feel especially alone in church, because many congregations tend to focus on families. Or maybe your church has a women's mentoring ministry—why not get involved there? Newer Christians can benefit from our faith journey. We can relate Bible verses that have uplifted us, prayers that God has graciously answered, and helpful resources. (And we can also tell them about our less-than-graceful life experiences, encouraging them to learn from our mistakes!)

Younger friend.

Often the richest relationships come from people we don't expect. Many older women don't realize how much a blessing a younger friend can be. Why not try to develop such a friendship? Ask God for the right partnership—and watch Him work. You might be surprised how much you can learn from someone born before your time.

Online friend.

I've been privileged to get to know dozens of awesome women by reading their blogs, responding to their e-mails, and chatting with them on Facebook. Sometimes, they've approached me, and other times, I've made the first move. But many of them have become very dear to me, because sometimes it's easier to be honest and vulnerable when you don't have to look a person in the eye. Many of these women write with a gut-level transparency that I appreciate and hope to emulate. Some of them are juggling way more kids than me, while homeschooling and volunteering at their church. I admire them and absolutely love it when life brings us together face-to-face, whether at a concert, conference, or through work-related travel.

Non-Christian friend.

As important as Christian friends are, we need non-Christian friends, too. They keep us in touch with the world.

Often, we surround ourselves with people just like us—and we miss out on wonderful friendships (not to mention opportunities for ministry). But don't just see a nonbelieving friend as a soul-winning prospect—respect them for who they are and all they have to offer.

Soul mate.

This is a kind of lifelong friend. A soul mate is a buddy who knows what you're going to say before you say it, because she's just like you. You don't have to ask her questions—you already know the answers. A soul mate is a comforting presence, someone you can turn to when you're down or exhausted. You can just "be" with this kind of friend, because she understands you so well. I'm grateful to have a soul mate in my husband, and also in a friend I met through a Christian drama group. My friend and I live four states away from each other, but I know whenever I call or e-mail, she'll be excited to hear from me. . .and she'll understand what I'm going through—whether I've found another gray hair or I'm about to pull my hair out over problems with my family.

Shared-interest friend.

Friends don't *have* to be soul mates—sometimes we just need a shared interest (kids, hobbies, spouses who work together, fellow walkers, widowers, or divorcees) to find common ground. These types of friends can provide small doses of sanity and "so I'm *not* the only one who feels like that!" relief in the midst of hectic schedules. They're also great encouragers—because they know mostly the good things about you! When we hit the proverbial wall, our weight keeps creeping up for no apparent reason, or a seemingly impossible work deadline looms, we need a pal who will say, "You're doing great!" or "Keep it up! I know you can do it!"

Although making and maintaining friendships—especially with a wide variety of people—can seem overwhelming, friends are also one of God's most wonderful gifts.

Yet, there may be times when we try to be a friend and are met with resistance or betrayal. As we get older, friendships may become more difficult. We have more issues to deal with, more complicated family problems, and our bodies rebel at all the wrong times. It can make a gal frustrated enough to put her hands up in the air and say, "Forget it!"

Take writer Michelle Van Loon and her husband, who long for good friends. But they feel like people their age have dropped out of church, and it's hard to find like-minded couples to befriend. "After our youngest child finished high school, we put the sprawling suburban Milwaukee ranch house in which we raised our three kids up on the market, and relocated to Chicago. My husband Bill and I began a search for a church near our new home. The search quickly alerted us to a surprising and under-reported trend."

Michelle noticed that there's a group quietly disappearing

from churches: middle-aged and older adults. She says, "Travel and health issues account for some of this. But also, most churches focus on younger families and couples with kids.

"Without kids as a connecting point, it was slow, hard, and lonely-going breaking into the social fabric of our mid-size new church. We have yet to really connect with some potential friends our own age."

That's tough. . .and sadly, too common. But I urge Michelle—and you—to prayerfully persist in looking for the friends God longs for you to have. Although it may be frustrating at times, the effort *will* pay off. And it's so worth it!

SETTING A COURSE

If you're struggling with hurts from past relationships, ask our heavenly Father for the willingness to forgive those who've mistreated you. (Start with praying for the desire—He will answer that—and give you the assistance you need to forgive later on.) When we nurse a grudge, the person we're really hurting is ourself. And the other person may not even know we're angry unless we tell them.

If we have the courage to, at least, forgive or, at most, lovingly confront those who've wronged us (or be open to receiving criticism from those we've hurt), we might see a miracle in the making. This happened to me once, when I had unknowingly been snobbish to a woman in my church. She was very hurt. Thankfully, she had the guts to call me and ask if I was mad at her. I said, "No!" Then, she called me onto the carpet (in a very loving way) about some less-than-stellar behavior I had inflicted upon her. And she told me she really wanted to get to know me better. I admired her so much for that! I apologized, and we became good friends.

What if you want to have friends, but you're just too busy with work, family, church, and other responsibilities? Here are a few ways to make friends a priority:

- *First, realize you need friends.* Consider them a necessity, not a luxury. You've heard it before, but it's true: We make time for things we believe are essential. And once you have good friends, spending time with them is addictive. You won't be able to stop!
- *Be bold, and approach someone new.* Nervous? Admit it. When you let people know that you're nervous but want to get to know them better, most of the time they'll immediately warm up and feel appreciated. Honesty is disarming—and charming. Really, what have you got to lose?
- *Make your friends a priority.* Try to remember their birthdays, or send them a note or e-mail when they're going through a tough time. Try not to cancel planned outings unless you absolutely have to. And let

them know—verbally and otherwise—how much you appreciate them.
- *Be diligent.* Use your time wisely, and don't give up if it's hard to get together (and try not to take it personally if a friend is busier than you). Make phone calls to friends while waiting for the doctor, or text or e-mail buddies while you're on a lunch break. If one person rebuffs your friendly advances, try again. If rebuffed again, consider it her loss and move on.

Joan Sparks has a model for friendship that others would do well to follow. She and three friends formed a group whose members call themselves the "Committee." They go shopping together, do lunch regularly, and take weekend trips as a group.

She says, "Ever shop for a bathing suit with a 'Committee'? We are ruthlessly honest about everything that we wear. If the 'Committee' says, 'that dress is *you*!' then you must buy the dress!"

But the "Committee" isn't just for fun. Joan notes, "Whenever there is a crisis, the 'Committee' circles the wagons and takes care of the person who is suffering. Fruit baskets, flowers, meals, all flow from the membership."

Now that's what I'm talking about!

Yet perhaps you struggle with having—or being—a friend because you've been hurt, or because you never had a role model for making and sustaining great relationships. Women can be very hurtful to one another, and some women actually feel more comfortable with men.

Which brings me to an important point regarding friendship—be careful, especially when you're with a group of women, not to gossip about other people or start husband bashing. Women are prone to get catty and complain-y when we're with a group of other women who "get" us.

Also, if you have a group of friends that regularly gets together for Bunco or lunch, try not to become too much of a clique. Is there a new person in your church or neighborhood? Invite him or her along. You might be surprised at what someone new can contribute. And no one can have too many friends!

If you've been hurt by gossip or cliquish behavior from other women, try to forgive them. And know that everyone makes mistakes, and friendships are still one of God's best gifts. Whatever your background, please don't let past experiences or personality differences cut you off from one of the most rewarding treasures God gave to the human race.

Let's face it. We're *all* just works-in-progress. But thankfully, in Christ, we can forgive and be forgiven.

It's not easy. In fact, it may be the most difficult thing Jesus asks us to do—especially if our disappointment and anger stems from abuse by friends or family members.

Forgiving doesn't mean letting people off the hook for what they've done. Wrong is wrong. Abuse is terrible, and God hates it.

Forgiveness doesn't mean that the people who have offended us were right, or even that they won't face judgment for their sins. It just means that we give up trying to punish the people who've wronged us with our silence, anger, or hatred. . .because in fact, when we hold on to those things, we're punishing ourselves. A lack of forgiveness can cause all sorts of health problems. Clinical psychologist Everett Worthington Jr., author of *Five Steps to Forgiveness: The Art and Science of Forgiving*, found that people who hold grudges have more stress-related diseases, less immunity, and worse rates of heart disease than folks who let go of their hurts.

In not letting go of the wrongs done against them, bitter people punish themselves. (This is one reason God commands us to forgive—He made us, and He knows how our bodies work!) Worthington found that people who let go of their anger and hurt have fewer episodes of depression, more stable marriages, and a better social network.

Think you can't forgive? Ask Jesus to help. At Calvary, He set the ultimate example for us, crying out to God for His Father to forgive those who were crucifying Him. Hebrews 4:16 says, "Let us therefore come boldly to the throne of grace, that we may obtain mercy and find grace to help in time of need" (NKJV).

In *Mean Girls All Grown Up*, Hayley DiMarco wrote, "How will we ever learn to forgive our enemies if we have no enemies? How will we ever learn perseverance if we never have anything to persevere through?"[11]

And don't forget that God has forgiven *us* completely. When Jesus died on the cross, God crucified our sins and won't hold them against us anymore. Hallelujah! First John 1:9 says, "If we confess our sins, he is faithful and just and will forgive us our sins and purify us from all unrighteousness" (NIV).

Forgiving and being forgiven are two of the secrets to an abundant life—and beautiful friendships.

Still unsure about whether you could be—or have—a great friend? Guess what—again, we have a perfect role model in Jesus Christ. He shows us what godly friendship is all about. He keeps His promises and sticks by us, because we're His family. He loves us through all kinds of weather, and His holiness shapes our own until we mirror Him. He consoles, cajoles, and convicts—all to make us more like Him.

When no one else knows what we're going through, Jesus does. When we feel abandoned or betrayed, He understands, because He's been right where we are. When our pals are too busy (or nonexistent), He has all the time in the world for us. And in His perfect timing, He will answer the desire of our heart for friends, and make us into the kind of friend everyone will long to have.

Jesus will never reject, betray, abandon, gossip about, forsake, or belittle us.

---

[11] DiMarco, Hayley, *Mean Girls All Grown Up: Surviving Catty and Conniving Women* (Grand Rapids, MI: Revell, 2005), 44–45.

That's not to say that He'll never allow us to be lonely. Sometimes He takes us away from our comfort zones (as in a job loss or a move to another city) so we have to depend on Him. In those times, He's our closest confidante, our provider, and our shelter. But here's the deal: He wants to be our best friend in the good times, not just the hard ones.

Bernard Meltzer, a radio host and media personality, once said: "A true friend is someone who thinks that you are a good egg, even though he knows that you are slightly cracked."

That's Jesus—our true friend, who created us and knows us inside and out. He sees our foibles, faults, and foolishness, and loves us anyway.

Now *He's* a good egg.

SMOOTH SAILING

Perhaps you wonder where in the world to start learning about how to be a friend. If so, the Bible is always a great place to land. Did you know the Word of God addresses friendships? *The Message* contains these practical pointers in Proverbs:

- *Keep your promises:* "Reliable friends who do what they say are like cool drinks in sweltering heat—refreshing!" (25:13).

- *Stick by your friends as though they're family:* "Friends come and friends go, but a true friend sticks by you like family" (18:24).
- *Revel in your differences:* "You use steel to sharpen steel, and one friend sharpens another" (27:17).
- *Don't take off when things get rough:* "Friends love through all kinds of weather" (17:17).

Meditate on these promises when you feel lonely, asking God to send refreshing, loyal, godly friends. And bask in His friendship—He's the one friend who "sticks closer than a brother" (Proverbs 18:24 NIV).

Chapter 7

INVEST IN WHAT MATTERS

A stockbroker urged me to buy a stock that would triple its value every year. I told him, "At my age, I don't even buy green bananas."
CLAUDE PEPPER

THE DRIFT

One of the biggest concerns of older women is in terms of money. . . . Will they ever have enough to retire on? Will Social Security go bankrupt? Will their investments go south, and, if they have children, have they saved enough for their kids' college education? Should they invest in real estate, stocks, or bonds? And if they have to work longer than they want to, will they be able to find a job they don't hate?

To be honest, I don't know a lot about investing money, but I do know a few commonsense principles about finances: Try to pay down debt, spend less than you make, and save for emergencies. But for helpful financial advice, I'll leave you to the Dave Ramseys, Ellie Kays, and Suze Ormans of the world.

We do know that God doesn't want us to worry about money (as hard as that is).

In the Sermon on the Mount, Jesus said to His listeners: "Therefore I tell you, do not worry about your life, what you will eat or drink; or about your body, what you will wear. Is not life more important than food, and the body more important than clothes? Look at the birds of the air; they do not sow or reap or store away in barns, and yet your heavenly Father feeds them. Are you not much more valuable than they? Who of you by worrying can add a single hour to his life?" (Matthew 6:25–27 NIV).

He goes on to say: "And why do you worry about clothes?

See how the lilies of the field grow. They do not labor or spin. Yet I tell you that not even Solomon in all his splendor was dressed like one of these. If that is how God clothes the grass of the field, which is here today and tomorrow is thrown into the fire, will he not much more clothe you, O you of little faith? So do not worry, saying, 'What shall we eat?' or 'What shall we drink?' or 'What shall we wear?' For the pagans run after all these things, and your heavenly Father knows that you need them. But seek first his kingdom and his righteousness, and all these things will be given to you as well. Therefore do not worry about tomorrow, for tomorrow will worry about itself. Each day has enough trouble of its own" (Matthew 6:28–34 NIV).

Although we may struggle a lot with this idea, the Bible contains numerous accounts of God telling us to trust Him to take care of us. And, if we look back on the past years, we know He always has.

He also asks us in His word, to give 10 percent (or more) of our income back to Him in the form of a tithe. And when we're obedient to do that, He more than meets our needs. He also builds trust in us, and shows up time and again, proving that you simply can't "out-give" God.

Martha, a single mom, says her mother is her role model because she has faithfully invested in the Word, her family, and in God's economy. Martha relates, "My mom at eighty-three looks at life so gracefully and loves so deeply! She is not the type of mother that gave her children everything they desired, but she gave us everything we needed. Her seven children, eighteen grandchildren, and eighteen great-grandchildren are prayed for daily by her—as is any other person who has a problem or concern. And tithing was something I saw her do regularly. If only ten dollars came in the mail and she had hardly any money, she would give that one dollar to the Lord and His work.

Like Martha's mom, Kathi has had more than her share of financial stress over the past five years. Numerous bouts of "budget cut" unemployment and a unique house situation that ended in foreclosure have forced her and her husband to dip heavily into what little retirement they'd accumulated through a generous 401(k) program at a former employer. She notes, "Now, our monthly finances are finally becoming a little more stable, but we are looking at a future with little retirement savings, and absolutely no credit available, as our credit score is so low it's practically off the charts. I'm assuming that I'll be working well past traditional retirement age, and even after that, will have to keep part-time employment in retail or something similar, just to live comfortably."

But she also says, "We've been very blessed with our health, and our children have had few difficulties, so what has gotten us through those five horrible years is the knowledge that money is not eternal and what *is* eternal—our kids, our family, our faith, our friends—is fine."

So how's your own investment strategy? Are you counting on worldly goods for your security, or do you place your hope at the feet of the only One who offers real wealth? Do you trust in a 401(k)—or in Jesus?

Remember, we won't take anything with us when we die. Psalm 49:16–20 says, "Do not be overawed when a man grows rich, when the splendor of his house increases; for he will take nothing with him when he dies, his splendor will not descend with him. Though while he lived he counted himself blessed—and men praise you when you prosper—he will join the generation of his fathers, who will never see the light of life. A man who has riches without understanding is like the beasts that perish" (NIV).

And we don't want to gain riches at the cost of losing the values we hold dear. But what if God did bless us with great wealth? Hopefully, we would pray for wisdom and try to be as generous as people like Rick Warren, the pastor/speaker/bestselling author who has given away 90 percent of his income over the last few years, much of it to fight poverty and AIDS in Africa.

BALLAST

As our life advances, we may want to concentrate more on giving than getting—and that includes nonmonetary types of investing. Because, as we get older, these methods of wealth-building are as important—if not more so—than putting our money in the right accounts. Proverbs 22:9 confirms this: "A generous man will himself be blessed, for he shares his food with the poor" (NIV).

There are three types of heavenly investing that will pay off big-time in terms of heavenly rewards: investing in others, investing in God's Word, and investing in His dreams for us.

Investing in others.

As mentioned in chapter 6, mentoring holds awesome rewards—for both the mentor and the mentee. Each time we invest in a relationship that consists of accountability, transparency, and encouragement, we are supremely blessed. The wealth of love, advice, and life experience that mentor-mentee women share can be astounding. And it can become addicting! Personally, I can't get enough of pouring my life into other women—or of them pouring into me.

One young woman I had the privilege of meeting with regularly was Chansin Bird, a beautiful senior in high school, who longed to write and wanted advice on pursuing her passion. At the time we met, I was an exhausted mother of a toddler, and I had left my zeal for the Lord somewhere between getting pregnant and struggling to parent a two-year-old with a crazy-high level of energy and precociousness.

Seeing Chansin's love for the Lord and her youthful desire to spread His love (especially to those nonbelievers in her immediate family) challenged and inspired me. Her passion for Christ reignited the spark I had let die. So even though she came to me for mentoring, she helped me grow in the Lord as much as—or perhaps more than—I helped her. And it's no wonder. Proverbs, the best advice book of all time, says, "As iron sharpens iron, so one man sharpens another" (27:17 NIV).

One woman who has mentored me—and countless others—is Ginny Thomas. She says, "If given a choice, I'd rather be with young ladies than women of my own age discussing menopause and Medicare. (Please don't tell my friends that!) As a pastor's wife, I had the privilege of having a fellowship group in my home to encourage young women in their marriages and as young mothers. Many of these girls are now grandmothers and are passing on their spiritual knowledge to the next generation. Isn't that what being a mother is all about?"

For the last couple of years, Ginny has been a mentor for MOPS (Mothers of Preschoolers) at her church. She says, "I have had the opportunity to personally mentor them and sometimes had the chance to lead them to the Lord. I was

INVEST IN WHAT MATTERS

married for fifty-three fantastic years to my sweetheart who still called me his bride before he went to be with the Lord six years ago. How I pray that I can extend the joy of marriage to my MOPS girls so that they will train these little future 'mothers' and 'fathers'! I wouldn't trade it for the world."

Mentoring is a biblical principle. From the front of the book to the back, we see men and women of God spurring on their fellow travelers with words of truth:

God mentored Adam as He walked with the first man in the garden.

The priest Samuel mentored Eli when the young boy came to live with him in the temple.

Nathan mentored David when the king went cuckoo and killed a man to hide his adulterous relationship with that man's wife.

Elijah mentored Elisha, Naomi mentored Ruth, Jesus mentored His disciples, Paul mentored Timothy, and Solomon has mentored the world through the book of Proverbs.

And in the book of Exodus, Moses mentored the children of Israel:

At one point early in their sojourn, the Israelites' enemies were in hot pursuit, and in front of them stood an enormous expanse of water. What were they to do? If they turned back, their rivals would surely kill them. To venture into the Red Sea meant certain death as well.

Understandably, they turned to their leader: "As Pharaoh approached, the Israelites looked up and saw them—Egyptians! Coming at them!

They were totally afraid. They cried out in terror to GOD. They told Moses, 'Weren't the cemeteries large enough in Egypt so that you had to take us out here in the wilderness to die? What have you done to us, taking us out of Egypt?' " (Exodus 14:11–12 MSG).

Like petulant children, the former slaves turned to the man in charge and whined. And before we go any further, perhaps we need to ask ourselves if we, at times, have done the same thing.

There we are. Stuck. Our enemies—self-doubt, fear, depression—are pursuing us. In front of us are the deep darkness of grief and the hard work of sanctification. To go forward requires a faith we don't have. To go back means losing all we've learned. So we complain to God, our mentors, our friends—basically anyone who'll listen.

"Lord, why haven't you answered my prayers?" we cry. "I thought You blessed those who seek You. I've been asking You for the same thing for months, even years. Don't You hear my prayers? Didn't You hear me when I said I'd had all I could bear? How long will You let me go on like this?"

Yet sometimes, God *allows* us to get to a "Red Sea" place in our lives in order to *show* His glory to us—just as He did for the Israelites. But He doesn't leave us alone in the meantime. Many times, He'll send us a mentor—an encourager to spur us on and give us guidance.

But sometimes we hate waiting. With a passion.

And the children of Israel were the same way. It's likely they didn't appreciate Moses' response to their little temper tantrum. He said: "Don't be afraid. Stand firm and watch GOD do his work of salvation for you today. Take a good look at the Egyptians today for you're never going to see them again. GOD will fight the battle for you. And you? You keep your mouths shut!" (Exodus 14:13–14 MSG).

Amazing! The Israelites' leader told them that they were getting a little too big for their britches—just what a godly mentor should do. He basically said, "Sit down, shut up, and let God work!" And can't you just see the Israelites' astonished faces and hear their incredulous replies: "What did he say? Be still and be quiet? A lot of good that will do!"

We often act the same way. God tells us to wait, and we decide that's not good enough. So we make ourselves miserable trying to solve the problem on our own. Instead, we should be still and listen to the Word and the wisdom of those godly encouragers God has placed around us.

Here's the sticky part: We may want a quick fix, while

God wants us to be refined and purified by a time of waiting for Him to act.

And here's the awesome part: God was with the Israelites, as He is with us today. He sent a mighty wind, which blew back the Red Sea until it made two walls. Then He commanded His children to move. And one by one, they resolutely set foot into the bottom of the ocean, marveling at the incredible sights on either side of them.

God will do the same for us. Whatever problems we have, we need only to listen to His wisdom—through the Word and others who follow Him closely—and obey His commands. We can be still, and allow the Lord to blow back the sea and blow us away with His miraculous deeds. He will make sure we arrive on dry land, and in doing so, He might just slay a few of those enemies we've been running from.

Investing in God's Word.

Dr. Marcia McQuity, who teaches education at Southwestern Theological Seminary, says, "Last semester I challenged my students in my parenting and faith development class to read Paul's letter to the Ephesians fifty times during the semester. About one third of the class accomplished the task. Some read the letter forty times, some twenty-five times. I read the letter fifty times. . .and learned so much!"

Marcia was impressed by the word *power* being used so many times throughout Ephesians. She says, "The letter also challenges us 'no longer to be children, tossed here and there by waves and carried about by every wind of doctrine' (4:14 NASB) and to 'not give the devil an opportunity' (4:27 NASB). The last chapter challenges us to put on the whole armor of God in order to resist the attacks from Satan. We resist him by reading the Bible and becoming like Christ, which means that we love God above all else and live each day walking in His ways, obeying His commands. As a result of reading the Bible, I pray every day, asking God to protect each of my children and grandchildren from the attacks of Satan."

In the book *It Is Enough*, the author, Bud Fray, tells a story about a professor at Oklahoma Baptist University who for twenty years read one complete Gospel each week. . .all four Gospels each month. The professor's son later said, "My dad was a man who lived like Jesus, talked like Jesus, became angry at the things that angered Jesus."

I pray that God continues to give me that kind of passion for His word, so that I can impart that love of the Word to those around me. Remember my mentee, Chansin? She had challenged me to "wake up" and get back to a fiery passion for God. To be honest, I regret spiritually sleepwalking through those years before I met her. And though God doesn't condemn me, I wonder what might have been. What had I missed? What lessons had I not learned? What lives had I not touched because I had been wrapped up in my own fatigue and frustrations?

Maybe you're like I was: a "good" Christian who gradually, almost imperceptibly, forgot what radical obedience looked like.

The good news is—it's never too late. God is an ever-patient parent who waits up all night to hear the key in the lock, only resting when His kids come home.

My friend Pam has learned to lean into God's Word and away from other things through a very unusual new hobby: reading a certain set of books. She says, "I have my teenage daughter to thank for introducing me to *Twilight* (Stephenie Meyer's bestselling novel about a love story between a vampire and a mortal). Pam flew through four hardbacks and two viewings of the *Twilight* movie, and she became as hooked as a rock-and-roll groupie.

Pam says it was pretty unnerving to find herself turning into a pop-culture fanatic in her forties, but she suspects it's because she is middle-aged that these stories are so compelling to her (and all the other aging "Twi-Hards" out there). Pam told me that she and her husband have reluctantly acknowledged that they're entering the season when "life stops giving you things and starts taking them away."

"We've already said good-bye forever to smooth skin, reliable vision, and, in Brent's case, almost a full head of hair!" Pam reports. This past year brought them additional loss and hardship, as dollar worries, divorce, disease, and death threatened from every angle. Pam kept hearing that marriages of people she cared about were becoming casualties of divorce. And funerals of several loved ones are looming on their horizon.

She admits that her traditionally optimistic nature is unequal to so much heartache: "For the first time in a very long time, I want to throw up my hands and cry, 'That's it! Life stinks! I give up!' "

But when Pam opened the pages of *Twilight*, everything that plagues our world was neatly reconciled with the stroke of a pen.

"*Twilight* is the ultimate escapist fantasy," Pam says. "Deep down I know that the source of my yearning is because I was not created for this world. Ultimately I was made for eternity, where life and love really do last forever. It is only natural that I should ache for the things of heaven."

In the end, Pam told me, the *Twilight* books only offer "distractions, not solutions." Though she thinks Stephanie Meyer is a truly gifted author, Pam knows it's silly to think an author can solve her dilemmas. For those answers, she must turn to the One who authored *her* life.

"I sense Him urging me to return to those pages He created just for me. Gently He chides me, 'If you spend all your time in someone else's book, you'll miss the very best parts of *your* story.' "

Are you missing the very best parts of *your* own story? Perhaps we all need to begin a holy quest, asking God for a daily renewal of passion for the Bible and His presence. As we consciously and consistently surrender our lives to Him, we'll discover the supreme riches of His grace and the sublime adventures He's calling us to. What better reward could there be?

Investing in God's dreams for us.

For the third and final type of investment, let's listen to the story of Marsha Marks, a forty-something author and publisher, who is investing in God's dreams for her—the unique story that He's written with her in mind. She is very vocal about her faith in wonderfully creative and accessible ways. As a former flight attendant, Marsha has shared the hope of Jesus in the airline industry, during her media appearances, and on her blog and Web site. And after writing several humor books, Marsha decided to do something crazy, if you look at it through worldly eyes. She pitched a sitcom—about her crazy life as a Christian flight attendant and author who feels "too worldly for the church and too churchy for the world"—to television executives.

Marsha wants to be the executive producer on this project, but everyone has told her that no one is going to go for that. So, she may have to raise the funding and produce the pilot herself, which she believes is possible. She says, "The Word says, 'What is impossible with men is possible with God' [Luke 18:27 NIV]. And I want this pilot to be funny and family-friendly so Christians can watch it with their young children. So, if I get the funding and backers myself, and shoot the pilot, and it goes well, then we can sell it and I can stay on as executive producer."

Marsha is boldly stepping forward in faith to realize God's dream for her life. What about you? What are your dreams? Have you given them up because you think you're too old to accomplish anything of worth?

Well, here's a little reality check for you:

- Sarah Bernhardt was 78 when she acted in her last stage performance.
- Sophocles was 89 when he wrote *Oedipus* at Colonus, one of his dramatic masterpieces.
- On the day of his death, at the age of 78, Galileo was said to be planning a new kind of clock that would tell time—in minutes and seconds, not just hours—using a pendulum swing instead of movement of water or sand.
- Mary Baker Eddy was 86 when she founded the *Christian Science Monitor*.
- Robert Frost was 88 when his last volume of poems, *In the Clearing*, was published.
- Winston Churchill was 79 when he received the Nobel Prize for Literature.
- Igor Stravinsky was 84 when he completed his last work, *"Requiem Canticles."*
- Charles de Gaulle was 75 when he was reelected

president of France.
- Pablo Picasso produced 347 engravings in his 87th year.

And last, but certainly not least:

- Grandma Moses received her last commission as an artist when she was 99.[12]

How's that for motivation? And don't forget one of the superstars of the 2008 Summer Olympics, Dara Torres, who was the oldest female swimmer in the history of the Olympic Games (at the relatively young age of forty-one). She came away from the games with three silver medals. Not bad for a gal who was called "Grandma" by all the young swimmers in Beijing!

Torres, whose memoirs are appropriately titled *Age Is Just a Number*, won the first of her twelve Olympic medals in 1984, a year *before* Michael Phelps was even born! Torres is now forty-two and the mother of a three-year-old daughter, Tessa Grace. Dara broke her first of three world records in 1982, at age fourteen, and she has retired from swimming and has come back three times. She is the first American swimmer to compete in five Olympics (despite sitting out in 1996 and 2004).

Torres is a role model for staying fit, aging gracefully, and

---

[12] Facts excerpted from *Splendid Seniors: Great Lives, Great Deeds*, by Jack Adler (Nashville, TN: Pearlsong Press, 2007). Used by permission.

pursuing your dreams.

Dara's dream of an Olympic comeback first hit her when she was months into her first, hard-won pregnancy. She returned to serious training while nursing her infant daughter and contending with her beloved father's long battle with cancer.

Talk about an inspiration!

So what's stopping you? Has Satan lied to you and told you that you'll never amount to anything, because you're "over the hill"? Do you feel worthless because you haven't pursued something God has laid on your heart? Do you think it's too late?

It's not, my friend! God gives us dreams for every stage of our lives, and His grace continually makes all things new. So tell the devil to back off! Claim the truth that God is for you, and that He is the author of dreams.

Another woman who epitomizes the forms of investing we've been discussing is the biblical heroine Rahab. She put her trust in God and invested in her family, His truth, and His dreams for her. But she didn't begin as an example of shining morality; on the contrary, she was the Heidi Fleiss of her day. Scripture tells us that she ran a house of ill repute (Joshua 2:1).

Jericho, a walled city, guarded the pass leading westward into the mountainous region of the Promised Land. Joshua and the children of Israel had been told by God that they were going to conquer Jericho. Its strategic location made its

Let the Crow's Feet and Laugh Lines Come

capture key to the invasion of the rest of the hill country.

The city where Rahab lived was a beautiful, well-watered oasis surrounded by desert. But it was also a center of perversity and debauchery. The people worshipped pagan gods, and the king didn't bow to the one true God, either.

Rahab had been told about Israel's God, as had the rest of Jericho. But Rahab took to heart the miracles she'd only heard about. When Joshua sent a couple of spies to survey the town, she gave them shelter. Risking her business and her very life, she also lied for them when the king's men came looking for them.

She told the men, "I know that God has given you the land. We're all afraid. . . . We heard how God dried up the waters of the Red Sea before you when you left Egypt, and what he did to the two Amorite kings east of the Jordan. . .We heard it and our hearts sank. . . . Now promise me by God. I showed you mercy; now show my family mercy" (Joshua 2:9–12 MSG).

The men agreed to spare her and her whole family when they conquered the city—and they kept their promise. Her faith provided them escape, and they provided safety for her during the battle for Jericho.

The remarkable thing about Rahab is that she, too, became part of the lineage of Jesus Christ. Matthew mentions Rahab (Matthew 1:5) as one of five women (along with Tamar, Ruth, Bathsheba, and Mary) in his first chapter's extensive genealogy of Jesus.

From harlot to heroine to ancestor of the Savior of the world. Wow.

Rahab saw her heavenly-minded investments pay off big-time after she clung to the truth about God and risked everything to follow His plan.

God wants us to do the same.

When enemies (financial worries, family troubles, health issues) threaten, He longs for us to cling to Him like a child clings to her mother. He wants to impart His wisdom to us, through the Bible and godly mentors. And when we allow Him to, He will give us far bigger—and far better—dreams than we could have ever imagined on our own.

Does it get you excited when you read about women like Marsha Marks, Dara Torres, or Grandma Moses? It should! Let it thrill you that women your age—and much older—have chosen to invest in mentoring, radical obedience to God's Word, and living out the Creator's plans for them. Allow those stories to inspire you and give you a passion for uncovering your own dreams and long-buried desires. Imagine what He can do with a heart and life that's completely surrendered. Dare to step out—with confident faith, not in yourself, but in His power working through you.

I pray that you and I will be like Rahab, who risked everything for the God she believed in, and in doing so, received an amazing return on her investment.

◯ SMOOTH SAILING

The investments we make in God's Word, other people, and the calling He's placed on our lives (and the results of those choices) are the only things that will follow us into eternity.

As Paul wrote to Timothy, his mentee: "Tell those rich in this world's wealth to quit being so full of themselves and so obsessed with money, which is here today and gone tomorrow. Tell them to go after God, who piles on all the riches we could ever manage—to do good, to be rich in helping others, to be extravagantly generous. If they do that, they'll build a treasury that will last, gaining life that is truly life" (1 Timothy 6:17–19 MSG). Here are some more truths to digest and remember:

- *Whoever loves money will never have enough money; whoever loves wealth will not be satisfied with it.*
  ECCLESIASTES 5:10 NCV

- *"No eye has seen, no ear has heard, no mind has conceived what God has prepared for those who love him."*
  1 CORINTHIANS 2:9 NIV

- *I was young and now I am old, yet I have never seen the righteous forsaken or their children begging bread. They are always generous and lend freely; their children will be blessed.*
  PSALM 37:25–26 NIV

- *"Don't store treasures for yourselves here on earth where moths and rust will destroy them and thieves can break in and steal them. But store your treasures in heaven where they cannot be destroyed by moths or rust and where thieves cannot break in and steal them."*
  MATTHEW 6:19–20 NCV

- *There has never been the slightest doubt in my mind that the God who started this great work in you would keep at it and bring it to a flourishing finish on the very day Christ Jesus appears.*
  PHILIPPIANS 1:6 MSG

- *"But me—who am I, and who are these my people, that we should presume to be giving something to you? Everything comes from you; all we're doing is giving back what we've been given from your generous hand. As far as you're concerned, we're homeless, shiftless wanderers like our ancestors, our lives mere shadows, hardly anything to us. God, our God, all these materials—these piles of stuff for building a house of worship for you, honoring your Holy Name—it all came from you! It was all yours in the first place! I know, dear God, that you care nothing for the surface—you want us, our true selves—and so I have given from the heart, honestly and happily."*
  1 CHRONICLES 29:14–17 MSG

Chapter 8

BECOME AUDACIOUS

"The future is as bright as the promises of God."
MISSIONARY HUDSON TAYLOR

THE DRIFT

Shortly after her sixtieth birthday, Liz met Jane Ray. Liz says, "At seventy-five, radiance surrounded Jane, and she became a dear friend who taught me to forget everything I knew about aging. Jane's life had not been easy, but she loved her Lord with an unfailing passion and served Him quietly with joy and delight."

"Jane's motto—and she practiced what she preached—was to 'Give thanks. In all things! No matter what!' Her primary mission in life was to encourage every person who crossed her path. Even on my dowdiest of days, Jane flashed me her gorgeous smile and said, 'Oh, my, Liz! You are beautiful today.' Every time, I blushed and said, 'Jane, you are sweet to say that.' And every time, Jane took me by the shoulders, drilled me with her piercing blue eyes, and stated, 'I am *not* nice at all, but I am absolutely honest!' "

Liz says that Jane didn't judge her, even on Liz's worst days. Instead, Jane Ray saw through the eyes of Jesus in every situation.

Liz's favorite memory of Jane was on the National Day of Prayer. At the end of the service on the steps of the county courthouse, the minister in charge thanked people for attending. Liz says, "In an instant, Jane began singing, 'Praise God from whom all blessings flow. . . .' And immediately, all of us lifted our voices with hers in thanksgiving. Twelve years later, I giggle to myself when I think of Jane."

Jane was living a radiant, joy-filled life. Don't you want that for yourself? You can have it! Jesus said in John 10:10 that He came to give us an abundant life. That doesn't mean our daily existence will be carefree, but rather that He will be with us during the tough times. And in the midst of the challenges aging brings, we can have joy. . .real, deep, lasting joy.

So let's leave behind our past behaviors, coping mechanisms, and the lies of the world and walk forward into these later years, trusting God to walk with us through the storms and give us the courage to be bold, brave women of faith.

Ladies, let's dare to be audacious! That's one of my favorite words. Dictionary.com and Thesaurus.com define *audacious* as adventurous, courageous, daredevil, daring, defiant, fearless, gutsy, hardy.[13] (Some negative words are also listed, such as *imprudent* and *arrogant*, but I want to concentrate on the positive aspects.)

Nancy is audacious. She wants to make sure she doesn't waste her life by not *truly* living. She related, "I want to live as [Henry David] Thoreau says in his classic *Walden*. . .'to live deliberately, to front only the essential facts of life, and see if I could not learn what it had to teach, and not, when I came to die, discover that I had not lived.' "

Audacious living is part of getting older gracefully. To me, *audacity* means living deliberately—waking up to what's right in front of us, and really living our lives, instead of just

---
[13] See dictionary.reference.com/browse/audacious.

watching from the sidelines or wishing we had a different set of circumstances. It's surrendering to God's plan and letting Him choose our path, so that one day we won't wake up and realize with regret that all our choices amount to nothing.

Wendy is also audacious. Recently, she and her husband went through a very difficult move, which involved financial hardship and the breakup of a business partnership. "I knew when we were going through all that, there was a reason. At one point, my husband said, 'Okay, Lord, exactly what am I supposed to be learning from this?' And I said, maybe it's not *us* that's supposed to be learning something—maybe God is using us to teach someone else something, and He knows that we're strong enough (in Him) to survive this. It won't bust our faith, or our confidence that He loves us and wants what's best for us, and the knowledge that He can turn *anything* ultimately into a blessing."

Wendy says that when you see God turning things into blessings over and over, it becomes obvious that God wants what's best for you and has great plans for you—even though those plans may not be immediately implemented. Then, she told me, when you do hit a bump in life, it starts to get really exciting. "I think, wow, okay, God, what is this one going to turn into? And if we choose to respond in the spirit, and not in the flesh, whatever happens will be for our ultimate good, and His ultimate glory."

That's the spirit of godly audacity—and the wisdom that comes from years spent walking with God. It's trusting Him as a child trusts her Father, because we know that Daddy won't send us anywhere by ourselves. It's the confidence that says, "I know You love me, and I know that if You're allowing me to be hurt, it's for a reason."

Of course, none of us likes to be broken. And yet, when we look back, we may realize that most of the times when we've had our pride shattered or our heart broken were the very times that God felt most real in our life.

But sometimes we don't always allow Him in our heart's door. Sometimes we say, "No, You won't!" when He asks permission (He is a gentleman, after all) to use a painful circumstance to change us. Sometimes we hold on to our pain and feed it, nurturing it like a helpless baby bird.

One afternoon when I was little, I came across a pitifully scrawny, sickly baby bird in our backyard. Having found it under a tree, I assumed it had fallen out of its nest and just needed some tender loving care. "You'll be as good as new!" I cooed to the little sparrow. My mom helped me find a box, which I lined with straw. I fed the bird water through an eyedropper and valiantly tried to nurse it back to health. Alas, it died before the evening was over.

Our ego is like that sparrow. We hold on to it stubbornly, refusing to admit how sick our souls are. We decorate a place in our hearts for the ego to rest, and justify our sins ("I'm not so bad," we coo to ourselves). We are pitiful and needy, but we don't admit that. Instead, we build ourselves up and try using the world's methods to make ourselves feel better. But God longs for us to look up, to give our souls over to Him for healing, because they are diseased. He wants to feed us with the Living Water—the Word of God, and the presence of Christ.

Not that it's easy. Our flesh loves worldly success. Left to our own devices, we struggle with wanting attention (which is why we sometimes dress in a way to show off our best assets, leaving modesty behind—am I right, ladies?). Look at the proliferation of reality shows, where people will do literally anything for their five minutes of fame.

Over and over, God asks us to lay down our selfish desires and dreams on the altar as we pray: "Whatever You want, Lord. Not my will, but Yours." Saying that is not fun, but I've learned the hard way that not surrendering is even less fun. A surrender-less heart is a joyless, peace-less heart.

The path to a childlike faith is not easy, it won't happen overnight. But let's keep striving for it—because the rewards are great.

Have you ever asked why God has allowed certain things in your own life, the lives of your friends, and in the world around you? Have you been asking, "Lord, why? I trusted You—and things turned out lousy."

If so, take time to listen to the answer. Instead of rushing into behaviors that have offered you comfort in the past—such as overeating, calling a friend to cry, or trying to make things happen—sit in the silence. Try to listen to what God might be saying to you in the midst of a tough time. Take time to be still.

At each juncture in our lives, He will continue to stretch us, push us, and take us to the next level in our faith-walk. It's not always easy, but it's always worth it. And in the midst of the journey, we find gifts—lots of them.

He gives us peace and joy in the midst of suffering. He gives us Christian friends and family members who spur us on to love and good deeds. And each day, when we're quiet and watchful, we may realize once more that He continually gives us eternal (not always material!) blessings at His right hand.

The question is, do we want to know more of Christ. . . and who He can be in us? Do we want life to become less about us and more about Him?

God will humble us, whether we ask Him to or not. But He'll only use humbleness in our lives if we allow Him to.

My pastor, John Hierholzer, says it this way:

God humbles those who exalt themselves, because they're not where they're supposed to be; they're not in touch with reality.

God exalts those who humble themselves, because they are where they ought to be—the place of need, the only place where someone can get rescued.

God is attracted to weakness, to brokenness, to

emptiness, to poverty, to lowliness, not because He wants to see us grovel, but because He wants to see us glorious, and that we simply cannot be, so long as we mistake human strength, human wholeness, human fullness, human wealth for the real thing.

Remember this: We have the choice to lick our wounds, rehearse our hurts, and become bitter, cynical people. Or we can let God take our what-in-the-world-was-I-thinking moments and make something out of them.

The question is, what kind of woman do you want to be?

Perhaps you are already audacious. That's terrific! Or perhaps that's something you may need to work on, like the main character in the movie *Hope Floats*. As the film begins, prim and proper Birdee Pruitt (played by Sandra Bullock) waits to find out what surprise a television talk show host has in store for her. In the next few moments, Birdee's entire world crashes around her as her "best friend" admits to an affair with Birdee's husband.

Birdee is devastated—and as a mom, she hurts for her daughter, too. The two move in with Birdee's mom in the small Texas town where Birdee grew up. Once she's there, Birdee falls apart, taking to her bed for days at a time.

Understandably, Birdee feels embarrassed about her very public talk show debut, horrified that her mother is still known as the town eccentric, and less than thrilled that her vision of happily-ever-after didn't turn out anything like she planned.

But through her mom's optimism and her daughter's need and own resilience, Birdee's spirits begin to rise, and life turns around. She sees the past for what it was—an illusion—and begins to create a future for herself in which old labels don't apply.

In one scene, Justin (played by Harry Connick Jr.) tells Birdee: "You used to be so audacious. People would stop and stare as you walked down the street. 'There goes that Birdee Calvert,' they'd say. I can still see that."

Justin's comments spark a turnaround for Birdee. She realizes that she is much stronger than she ever thought she was, and that she has something to offer the world.

Hope Floats reminds us that with God, we are much more special than we believe, and that through His strength, we, too, can be audacious.

What else does being audacious mean? It means having a confidence and boldness about life. The authentic kind of audaciousness (not a put-on version, where we build ourselves up in order to look better to others) comes from inside. It's born deep in the heart of the woman who fully trusts the One who created her.

Audacious women pursue their dreams of writing, traveling, or playing an instrument, because they've always wanted to do it—and that's reason enough.

They let their hair go gray and wear less makeup, because they're comfortable in their own skin.

They join an amateur team in their favorite sport and have the most fun they've ever had.

They take ballroom dancing lessons—by themselves.

They wear their favorite clothing without caring what anyone thinks—because having God's approval is all that matters to them. They know Jesus lives in them, and so they believe with all their heart that He says to them, "You are my [daughter], whom I love; with you I am well pleased" (Luke 3:22 NIV).

When faced with a crisis, like a parent's or child's illness, they surround themselves with friends, gird themselves with scripture, and refuse to cower in a corner.

They take job loss as an opportunity to reinvent themselves. Yes, they feel scared—but they don't let fear (or Satan's lies) defeat them.

When they feel sad, they cry and eat a little chocolate, and then they pick themselves up and get right back into living the life God gave them, bravely playing the cards they've been dealt.

They're women like Davina, who works two jobs and has survived breast cancer and two divorces, but realizes that God has never let her go hungry or miss a mortgage payment—and she's thankful!

Audacious women are our heroes.

They exude gratitude, joy, and hope. They are fearless in their second act of life, and they "shine like stars in the universe" (Philippians 2:15 NIV).

Another audacious woman is my mom, Susie Ratliff. After having a complete hysterectomy, Mom never regained her strength. She says, "The doctor told me some women grieve after surgery. Dismissing that statement, I just tried to focus on getting better. Instead, I got worse. Within a year and a half I was diagnosed with probable MS. Pain began to plague me, and I often felt that hot lava was coming out of my skin. Headaches hit with a vengeance. My husband rushed me innumerable times to the emergency room for painkilling shots for relief."

But no one could find out what was wrong. Doctors ran every conceivable test, and test results for MS were never conclusive. During that time, Mom had to rest from four to eight hours a day because of severe fatigue. She says, "God and my family were my greatest strength and comfort. I received the Bible on tape and would listen for hours every day. What great solace those scriptures were!"

She also found the *Streams in the Desert* books by Mrs. Charles E. Cowman and says, "Those books were a godsend to me. Every time I was really low (and there were *lots* of those times), her devotionals brought me hope. Only God could have had her write in 1937 what I needed to hear, over fifty years later."

At one point during her lengthy, mysterious sickness, she couldn't take it anymore. She started crying and begging God, "Please help me. You have led us through every step. Why can't someone find out something?" And she believes God was just waiting for her to say she couldn't go any further on her own. He brought the right doctor into her life, and she was ultimately healed—though she had to do a lot of hard work, as well.

That's audacity.

She says, "God has been there at every turn, guiding, directing, pushing, and sometimes pulling me toward the goal He has in sight for me. What that is exactly, well, I'll just have to be patient, wait, and find out. But what a ride it has been up to now!"

Getting older is an adventure, isn't it? And with God at the helm, even though we never know what lies around the bend, we can be assured that He has our best interests at heart.

The apostle Peter, went through several adventures—some of them not so fun—in the first century. Peter, who suffered from foot-in-mouth disease, was a fisherman by trade, left his nets to follow Christ, and saw amazing miracles during his first few weeks with the Messiah. Jesus had a special fondness for Peter, and He made the brash, lovable guy one of the men in His inner circle.

In fact, Peter harbored such great hopes for his future as a right-hand man to the King of the Jews that he blatantly refused to allow Jesus to talk about His upcoming crucifixion. In Matthew 16:21–27, Jesus tried to tell the disciples what would happen to Him, but Peter cried out, "Never! This will never happen to You, Lord!" (author's paraphrase).

I can almost see the big guy grabbing an imaginary sword and swinging it around. Perhaps Peter thought, *I won't let anyone touch You—You're my friend!* Or maybe, *Over my dead body! I have big plans for Jesus and the rest of us. He's going to usher in a new kingdom for the Jews—and I won't lose my place in that.*

Whatever Peter's thought processes were, he couldn't see the proverbial forest for the trees. He focused on the immediate repercussions of Jesus being captured and killed, while Jesus had God's redemptive plan in mind.

And what was Jesus' surprising (and volatile) reaction to His friend's forceful pronouncement? In verse 23, He practically yells: "Get behind me, Satan! You are a stumbling block to Me! You don't have in mind the things of God, but of men!" (author's paraphrase).

Can't you just see Peter shrinking back in discouragement, hugging himself with his cloak, and choking back tears as the group of disciples walked on?

Peter probably thought he was doing the right thing. Jesus' reply seems harsh to us, but we have to remember that He sees and knows all. He discerned Peter's heart-motives. . . whether grandiose, selfish, or carnal.

Peter's audacity served him well at times, but in other

instances, it brought only humiliation and shame. But every time Peter messed up, our gracious heavenly Father forgave Peter's sin. In fact, He turned the fisherman's life around. A few books later in the New Testament, we see Peter preaching with abandon and serving as an instrument in the conversion of thousands of people.

Peter could have become angry and bitter, refusing to forgive himself or to accept Jesus' offer of forgiveness. He could have stayed in his house, afraid of the government that had the early Church in its sights for persecution, prison, and worse. But, in faith, he stepped forward in courage.

Peter looked up and grasped the enormity of God's plan and the smallness of his own shame. He chose the narrow way. He became a warrior.

And we can do the same. Whatever our situation, and whatever ways we've chosen to cope before, we can allow God to turn our embarrassment, sin, and shame into something beautiful.

That's what being truly *audacious* is all about.

The Red Hat Society, which encourages women to wear red hats with purple clothing, is based on the poem "Warning" by Jenny Jones. The Red Hat Society is a national organization whose members join local chapters in order to lunch, chat, and travel with like-minded women. They have a common purpose: to greet their older years with humor and verve.

With chapter names like the Red Hattitudes, Bodacious

Beach Babes, and Long Tall Sallies, the Red Hat women and their attitudes about aging definitely come to mind when we think of the word *audacious*.

BALLAST

So how do you really become audacious—in the best sense of the word? First, stop thinking that nice girls don't rock the boat, and instead become bold women for Christ. If you were raised in church or in the South (or both), you were probably taught by word or example that "good girls don't make a scene." And although that may be good advice for doing well in school or for not disturbing a worship service, it's not applicable for modern Christian women.

A local church recently had this saying on their marquee: BE NICE. Every time I would drive by, I thought, *No! No! No!*

Being nice is not a bad thing, so I couldn't express in words why I was so ticked off at the sign—and then I remembered something Mike Yaconelli once wrote that resonated with me. He complained that Christians had gotten off track and that the most important issue of our time was not political or even moral. Yaconelli lamented that believers had simply lost their "astonishment." He said, "If Christianity is simply about being nice, I'm not interested. . . . I'm ready for a Christianity that 'ruins' my life, that captures my heart and makes me uncomfortable. I want to be filled with an astonishment which is so captivating that I am considered wild and unpredictable and...well...dangerous. Yes, I want to be 'dangerous' to a dull and boring religion."[14]

Amen, and amen! How many hundreds of times in your life have you bitten your tongue instead of saying something you felt strongly about? Was it because you were concerned more with the approval of men than obeying God's call?

You know what? Jesus' one concern was glorifying God, and making Him known. (*God, help us be more like that!*)

That's the focus of Rebekah Montgomery. Her life hasn't been easy, but she has found great strength from the call God has placed upon her life. With all her heart, she longed to serve God. But she says, "I didn't suppose God would ever open up a ministry for me. See, I was a woman, and according to many people, women were not supposed to do anything in the church except cook the food for potluck dinners and clean up afterward. My parents didn't subscribe to this interpretation of the scriptures, but so many did that I realized if I were to exercise the gifts God had given me, I would be the target of a great deal of criticism."

But little by little, God showed Rebekah in the scriptures exactly what He had called women to do. He showed her Mary, who washed the feet of Jesus. And He showed her Martha, "who served food to Jesus at first-century potlucks."

---

[14] From *Dangerous Wonder*, by Mike Yaconelli, New Edition edition (Peabody, MA: NavPress, 2003), quoted on www.youthtrain.com/html/resources/book_reviews/book_review_brown9.php.

She says, "Then there was Mary Magdalene and others who supplied Jesus with financial help. Deborah led, inspired, and judged. Miriam led music. Dorcas clothed widows and orphans. Lydia networked. Priscilla instructed Apollos. The woman at the well evangelized her village. Jesus didn't consign these women to work only in the nursery and hold babies: He reserved that extra special job for Himself."

But most of all, God pointed out to Rebekah the women who stood at the foot of the cross and witnessed His horrible death. These women prepared His body for burial and then assembled the spices to return on Sunday so they wouldn't break the Sabbath. They were the first to realize that the tomb was empty.

Rebekah says, "These were the women Jesus told to tell Peter and the disciples that He was risen—and that was precisely the job I felt called to do: to tell the world that Christ was risen."

She concluded if He had called her to a ministry within the church, He would open the doors for her so that others would recognize her call, too—and that's what has happened. She notes, "The discovery of God's call on my life has been a joyous adventure. He has allowed me to share the Good News of Jesus' resurrection in a variety of ways, from Bible school for underprivileged inner-city children to wealthy, upper crust matrons, from seminary-trained pastors to illiterate Haitians, from babies to senior citizens."[15]

---

[15] Copyright 2007 by author/speaker Rebekah Montgomery (http://www.rebekah-montgomery.com).

SMOOTH SAILING

So whatever storm you're going through—whether you're brokenhearted, dealing with career struggles, attempting to live with illness, queen of foot-in-mouth disease, or confused about your role in ministry—know that God's plans for you are good.

He wants to take all our talents, quirks, and weaknesses, and create something beautiful. He longs to make us into red hat–wearing, joy-sharing, trusting-Daddy-with-all-our-heart women of God.

The only question is, will we let Him?

Here are a few verses for you to meditate on and/or memorize:

- *"The thief comes only to steal and kill and destroy; I have come that they may have life, and have it to the full."*
  JOHN 10:10 NIV

- *Everyone will share the story of your wonderful goodness; they will sing with joy about your righteousness.*
  PSALM 145:7 NLT

- *Then he said to them, "Go your way, eat the fat, drink the sweet, and send portions to those for whom nothing is prepared; for this day is holy to our Lord. Do not sorrow, for the joy of the LORD is your strength."*
  NEHEMIAH 8:10 NKJV

- *"He will once again fill your mouth with laughter and your lips with shouts of joy."*
  JOB 8:21 NLT

- *You have made known to me the path of life; you will fill me with joy in your presence, with eternal pleasures at your right hand.*
  PSALM 16:11 NIV

- *Let your hope make you glad. Be patient in time of trouble and never stop praying.*
  ROMANS 12:12 CEV

- *And we pray this in order that you may live a life worthy of the Lord and may please him in every way: bearing fruit in every good work, growing in the knowledge of God, being strengthened with all power according to his glorious might so that you may have great endurance and patience, and joyfully giving thanks to the Father, who has qualified you to share in the inheritance of the saints in the kingdom of light.*
  COLOSSIANS 1:10–12 NIV

Chapter 9

GIGGLE, DANCE, AND SING

With mirth and laughter let old wrinkles come.
MERCHANT OF VENICE, WILLIAM SHAKESPEARE

I am having the darnedest time looking in the mirror. Every time I do, no matter what mirror it is, I see my mother. How can this be? I am still a kid, right? How can I be seeing my mother? Oh, wait a minute. I am now a senior citizen. No, I am a kid. No, I am not sure. I am both at the same time.

Let me try to figure out how this happened. . .or when.

Somewhere along the way, I grew up. Or I grew out or outgrew. Or I grew wiser, or more foolish. Or, what happened?

Let me go look in the mirror. Or let me not, because then I will see my mother again in my mirror.

It goes fast, this life.

Perhaps I should just live it!

PATRICIA BERLINER, LICENSED PSYCHOLOGIST

With God's help and by His grace, we can have the joy we long for. On her hilarious blog, author Mary Pierce said, "I checked my birth certificate. I'm exactly as old as God intended me to be, given the date of my birth. (Who am I to argue?) But I'll admit it. I'm slowing down a bit. I *am* more interested in oat bran these days than wild oats. More tempted to hit the recliner than the ski slopes."

She says her list of "Things I Want to Do in Life" is about equal to the list of "Been There, Done That." And she's okay with that. She's accomplished some things and accepted many others. And she's learning that what really matters is not the "stuff" and status young people try so hard to acquire. She's decided that what counts are the people who bless us, the love and laughter they give us, and the hope that faith brings. And she says that perspective and peace are the gifts time offers us, if we are willing to accept them.

Mary declares, "To the youngsters out there I say, 'Enjoy it while you've got it!' To the rest of us I say, 'We're in this together. We're getting older but *we're not done yet*! If ever we needed love and laughter and each other, it's now. So peace, baby, and please pass the shredded wheat!"

Mary's got a great attitude. And she's not the only person who has gotten cheerier about getting older. Researchers at the University of Chicago reported that we actually get happier as we age. In a study cited in *Quick and Simple* magazine, 24 percent of twenty-something Americans reported being very happy, and the numbers kept growing, with the contented lot increasing 5 percent every decade.[16]

Why is it that the actual statistics are the complete

---

[16] From *Quick and Simple* magazine, June 10, 2008, issue, page 19.

opposite of what the media and culture tell us? If we listened to television reporters and read the latest fashion magazines, we'd believe the lie that aging is terrible and should be avoided at all costs. (And since we can't avoid it, we might as well deny it, right?) But as we've discussed, those are lies from Satan.

Instead of finding that misery follows them into old age, many women are discovering joy in the journey. Multitalented media personality Linda Goldfarb says that when she was seventeen, her biggest concern was finding Mr. Right. At the age of twenty, it was, "How do I raise a baby when I'm still one myself?" When she turned twenty-eight, her biggest concern was how to get rid of Mr. Wrong and start looking again for Mr. Right. (Actually, she wasn't sure she wanted to look for anyone. . .so she didn't, but, eventually, he found her.)

Linda says, "The winded feeling that overtook me while blowing out the candles on my thirtieth birthday was nothing compared to the empty feeling inside as I wondered why God thought I needed to experience the loss of an unborn child. When thirty-eight rolled around, I found myself rolling into the maternity ward with my fourth child. Imagine, one starting college and one at the breast! I cried for a week, carrying around a pregnancy test I thought for sure would change because there was no way this late in life I could be pregnant."

Ladies, we have a God with a funny bone. At forty-two Linda was concerned about being on the road too much, as she encouraged literacy across the United States with a theater group while her husband stayed at home with their children. She said she got reminded often that, "A woman's place is in the home." And she tried to explain that to her husband and kids quite often, but it seemed she was always breaking up moments of laughter, trying to remind them they needed to miss her. Again, God's plans were much bigger than her concerns.

Now, says Linda, "At fifty-two, my ministry is launching globally with web-TV and an online live radio show, I have three wonderful grandkids, I work out three days a week with my hubby and fourteen year old boy, and because of His faithfulness, my biggest concern today is, 'Wow! What is God going to do next?!'"

Why not adopt such a hopeful attitude? After all, the scriptures are full of His promises for us—7,487 of them, to be exact. Why not choose to trust in the validity of them? *All of them.*

What if we decided that Isaiah 46:4 was true: "Even to your old age and gray hairs I am he, I am he who will sustain you. I have made you and I will carry you; I will sustain you and I will rescue you" (NIV)? I'd bet we would not worry so much about the future and what difficulties life holds for us, because we'd be convinced that God would sustain and carry us.

What if we clung to 1 Thessalonians 5:24: "Faithful is He who calls you, and He also will bring it to pass" (NASB)?

Maybe we would stop trying to make things happen on our own, and instead trust God's timing.

What if we hung on to Joshua 23:14 with all our hearts: "Now behold, today I am going the way of all the earth, and you know in all your hearts and in all your souls that not one word of all the good words which the LORD your God spoke concerning you has failed; all have been fulfilled for you, not one of them has failed" (NASB)? Perhaps we wouldn't stay up at night with an upset stomach, fretting over things we can't control.

How would it change us if we passionately believed Psalm 121:3–4: "He will not allow your foot to slip; He who keeps you will not slumber. Behold, He who keeps Israel will neither slumber nor sleep" (NASB)? I'd bet we'd take more risks and allow God to lead us into unfamiliar territories, instead of hunkering down in our small, safe corners of the world.

And what would our lives look like if we decided to literally take God at His word in 1 Corinthians 10:13: "No temptation has overtaken you but such as is common to man; and God is faithful, who will not allow you to be tempted beyond what you are able, but with the temptation will provide the way of escape also, so that you will be able to endure it" (NASB)? It's certain we would find more contentment in the midst of our difficulties.

How would hanging our hat on God's Word (and not just skimming, sort of digesting and half-believing it) affect our

Let the Crow's Feet and Laugh Lines Come

choices? Our peace quotient? Our sanity?

As the hourglass sands of our lives slowly ebb away, we find ourselves seeing something clearer than we've ever seen it before—God can be trusted. He has never lied to us. He has never, ever left us—not for one iota of a millisecond. And He has given us the grace to endure and overcome things we never dreamed we'd have the strength to survive.

And it's not because of anything good in us. It's all because of Him.

Along with God's presence, strength, and grace, He has given us another amazing gift: the choice of seeing the positive, the joyful, the humorous side of life—in good times and bad.

Aging is a *lot* more fun if we decide to laugh about it. We have the choice to say, "Oh, well," instead of making a big deal out of everything. Some things are big deals, and some aren't. It's important to know the difference. Because if we can't laugh at ourselves, we'll miss a lot of good stuff in life.

Learning to laugh at ourselves is the first step in allowing God to transform our major difficulties—and our minor aches and pains—into something precious. We can choose to laugh at ourselves when we lock ourselves out of our cars—twice in two days. We can chuckle at ourselves when we walk into a room and stop dead in our tracks, wondering not just what we came *in* for, but how we actually *got* there. We can quietly snicker at ourselves—once we get over the initial embarrassment—when we accidentally walk into the men's room instead of the women's.

Do people laugh with us? Hopefully. Regardless of what other people think about us (or say behind our backs) when we royally mess up, we feel better when we laugh.

And laughter has amazing health benefits. Dr. Lee Berk and Dr. Stanley Tan of Loma Linda University in California have studied the effects of laughter on the immune system. They've concluded that laughing does amazing things to the body—such as helping to decrease blood pressure, increase flexibility, reduce stress, and build up the immune system. Laughter also triggers the release of endorphins, the body's natural painkillers, and produces a general sense of well-being. For those of you who hate exercise, scientists have found that a belly laugh is equivalent to "an internal jogging." Laughter can provide good cardiac conditioning, especially for those who are unable to perform physical exercises. Frequent belly laughter even empties your lungs of more air than it takes in—similar to deep breathing.[17]

Martha Bolton is a humor author and one of our aging role models. In one of her books on getting older, *Didn't My Skin Used to Fit?* she wrote:

It happened at the post office near my house. I had driven there to mail a letter, and as soon as I got out of my car, this guy started howling and making wolf calls at me.

---

[17] See www.getreadyforlove.com/Love%20Sources/lsbenefitsoflaughter.htm.

They were loud, they were rude, and they were annoying. I walked to the post office entrance, trying my best to ignore his junior high behavior, but it was becoming increasingly more difficult.

Finally, I'd just had it. I was ready to give him a piece of my mind or at least shoot him a look that said exactly what that piece of mind was thinking. But when I turned to glare in his direction, I saw something totally unexpected. That howling wasn't coming from a man. It was coming from a dog—a very large dog upset about being left in a very small car.[18]

Martha says she was laughing so hard at herself when she stepped into the post office, the clerks must have thought she was crazy. But she couldn't help it! She had thought she was attracting the unwanted advances of a man, when she was merely attracting the attention of an impatient dog!

Martha says that now, when she hears someone make some sort of verbal advance at her, she turns to look before she starts judging: "The next whistle I hear might be coming from a parrot, and it's not easy to press harassment charges against fowl."

Speaker Suzie Humphreys is a vivacious redhead who crosses the country, speaking to groups of all sizes. With

---

[18] Martha Bolton, *Didn't My Skin Used to Fit?* (Grand Rapids, MI: Bethany House, 2000), 141–42.

obvious joy, Suzie told one audience of women story after story of red-faced moments, cringe-worthy decisions, and heartbreaking life experiences. Yet, through it all, she laughed. She "saw the flip side" of pain—and encouraged her fellow females to do the same.

After her doctors diagnosed her with an early stage of breast cancer, Suzie says, "I told them, let's take the thing off! At my age, no one's asking to see it anyway. Besides, I'm wearing a 38 long."

Suzie says, "When you're laughing, you're in the middle of a holy moment. You can't be afraid or worried when you laugh. You're perfectly at peace."

Some people [laugh at themselves] naturally, and others need to be taught. You have to look at life like it's a situation comedy."

If we take a step back, we'll discover that our lives are full of quirky characters, irritating conflicts, and maddening delays. And while our problems don't always resolve in thirty minutes or less, we can ask God to give us a new perspective on them. If we picture our lives through the lens of grace, we can almost always find something funny. So let's provide our own laugh track!

Yet, there will be times when we experience suffering. We may undergo depression, dozens of health problems, the death of loved ones, and other devastating losses. They are all very real and excruciatingly painful times.

But there are seasons for everything. As Ecclesiastes 3:1–2, 4 says: "To everything there *is* a season, a time for every purpose under heaven: A time to be born, and a time to die. . .a time to weep, and a time to laugh; a time to mourn, and a time to dance (NKJV)."

Give Christ access to all your wounded, scary places, and you *will* (in His time) experience freedom and joy. He is Jehovah Rapha, "the LORD, who heals" (Exodus 15:26 NIV). He is also the Great Physician. God wants to heal *you*. He wants you to laugh and dance and sing—not just in heaven, but here on earth.

He is for you. He is with you. He loves you more than you can imagine.

In Isaiah 55:2 and 12, God says: "Listen carefully to Me, and eat what is good, and let your soul delight itself in abundance. . . . For you shall go out with joy, and be led out with peace; the mountains and the hills shall break forth into singing before you, and all the trees of the field shall clap their hands" (NKJV).

Singing—out loud—is one of the best ways to get out of a funk. So what if you can't sing well? Sing in the shower, in your car—or with your friends. Plan a crazy karaoke party, and have everyone dress up as their favorite entertainer. Don't be afraid—be audacious!

Consider Cher, Madonna, Bette Midler, Aretha Franklin, and Tina Turner. Though we absolutely shouldn't model our lifestyles after them, they prove that aging doesn't have to mean hanging up our microphone, or any of the passions God's given us.

Just because the media implies that older people can't do much (and when they do, it doesn't really matter) doesn't mean it's true!

What if the thought of singing gives you hives? Well, if you're feeling blue, or out of steam, you might try spending time with another one of God's natural antidepressants: children. Kids laugh naturally and with abandon. Perhaps a child's propensity for merriment is one of the reasons Jesus rebuked His disciples when they wanted to shoo children away from Him. Remember what He said? Basically: "Listen, fellas, leave these kids alone. They are special, I love them, and guess what? The kingdom of heaven belongs to them" (Matthew 19:14, author's paraphrase).

Don't you know the disciples had a few things to say about that—at least among themselves? Back in Jesus' day, if you weren't a man, you were pretty much scum. Men saw women and children as little more than property (sadly, they're still looked at that way in certain parts of the world). But freely and scandalously, Jesus adored children.

Jesus talks about the kingdom of heaven belonging to children because they don't have our grown-up hang-ups. They're guileless, playful, and quick to laugh at themselves. Kids get back up when they fall and try again (just watch a baby learning to walk, and you'll see what I'm talking about).

Now adults, we'll attempt something once—or maybe twice. Then most of us give up. We use all sorts of excuses. See if these phrases sound familiar:

- It's too hard.
- I'm too old.
- That's not my gift (a favorite among Christians).
- I don't feel led (another Christian-ese statement that might or might not be true).
- They'll laugh at me.
- I'm praying about it (a good thing, but not when it's said as a pain-avoiding pious proclamation).
- I don't have the time/money/resources.
- I can't go through that again.
- It hurts too much.
- God won't give me what I can't handle. (This is not necessarily true, and is misquoting the Bible. Sometimes He pushes us beyond our limits so we'll lean hard into His strength.)
- I'm too tired.

So what are *your* excuses? What are you afraid to try? Or to try again?

Ladies, maybe we need to pray that God will renew our hearts and give us a childlike spirit so we can look at life

Giggle, Dance, and Sing

with hope and optimism again. We *are* still children—God's children.

Childlike spirit abounds in the movie *13 Going on 30*. Jennifer Garner's character, Jenna Rink, suffers extreme humiliation at her thirteenth birthday party, and she makes a wish to skip adolescence and go straight to adulthood.

Magically, Jenna's wish comes true, and she finds herself transported to the year 2004, where she's thirty years old, wildly successful, beautiful, popular, and (to her horror) a terrible person. Jenna has money, a great job, and fabulous clothes, but nothing of eternal value. Worst of all, she's lost touch with her childhood best friend, one of the only kids who was kind to her during her preteen years.

In one scene, which occurs at a boring work party, Jenna livens things up by getting her fellow employees to do the Thriller dance, to Michael Jackson's song of the same name. And after her co-workers get over their initial reluctance, they have a great time.

By the end of the movie, Jenna Rink, a dorky teen trapped in a woman's body, figures out what's important: friends, family, and being true to herself. It reminds us that if we take ourselves a *lot* less seriously, the world *won't* fall apart.

In fact, why *shouldn't* we act more like a kid? Why *not* swing on swing sets? Why not eat more ice cream? Why not do the Thriller dance? Why be scared of falling on our faces? And the most important question of all: What's the worst thing that could happen?

If you want to learn to laugh at life and yourself, and you don't have a child, grandchild, or niece, borrow one—any mom will be glad to let you take her kids off her hands for a while. Or just observe a young child's behavior by helping out in the church nursery. It will provide you with a bird's-eye view of a young person's outlook on life.

When we begin to see our world through a child's eyes, we become more observant of our surroundings. Mud puddles become lakes to jump into, and piles of dirt become castles. Ordinary things become filled with wonder and excitement.

Children see things in a different, more creative way. One child looked at a fresh cherry and asked his mom, "Mommy, when I eat the cherry, can I eat the antenna, too?"

As adults, we sometimes lose the ability to see the world with wonder. Instead of playing "make-believe," we get wrapped up in "shoulds" and "if only's." To a child, anything is possible. God is in charge, and He can do big things! A young person's presence can remind us that God as Creator has given us a wonderful universe to explore. Every day is a new opportunity to learn, laugh, and love! He makes all things new.

Of course, being with children can also remind us that we've crossed over into adulthood. Author Kathi Macias had no idea she had crossed the great "generation gap" until one of the publishers she worked with called and made her an interesting proposition. "We have just contracted with former football great Rosey Grier to publish a collection of Christian athletes' testimonies," the publisher said. "We need a writer to work with him. Are you interested?"

Interested? That was the understatement of the year! Not only was Kathi of the generation that clearly remembers that Rosey served as bodyguard to Senator Robert Kennedy and helped catch the senator's assassin, but she was also a football fan. She quickly accepted and immediately called her oldest son, Al, then in his early twenties and a huge football fan—or so she thought—to tell him the news. *Surely he will be impressed!* Kathi mused.

"You'll never guess who I'm going to be doing a project with," Al's mom announced to him as soon as he answered the phone. When Al inquired as to the identity of the mystery person, Kathi crowed, "Rosey Grier!"

After a brief moment of silence he asked, "Who's she?"

Kathi knew at that moment that she was no longer young—no longer hip or with it or anything else cool, for that matter. "True," she says, "I wasn't *old* old, but I was quickly heading in that direction. I mean, please, even my mother, who at that time was nearly seventy, knew who Rosey Grier was, and she'd never watched a football game in her life!"

Kathi and Rosey eventually did two projects together.

Let the Crow's Feet and Laugh Lines Come

She says, "I used that time to transition (as gracefully as possible!) from the 'young and restless' to the 'middle-aged and comfortable.' And now, nearly twenty years later, as I take advantage of Senior Discount Day at Kmart and Denny's, I'm still learning about seasons—remembering past ones with a hint of nostalgia, appreciating current ones with joy, and anticipating future ones with eager excitement. Why? Because all of God's seasons are good, and He can use us regardless of which side of the generation gap we're living in!"

Kathi's attitude is terrific, as well as the fact that she didn't take her kids' comments too personally. . .or herself too seriously.

Did you know that the mere thought of children caused one biblical woman to laugh? Her name was Sarah, and she was near the ninety-year mark. She and her husband Abraham—no spring chicken himself at one hundred years young—had not been able to have children together, though the Lord had promised them numerous offspring.

In Genesis 18, the scriptures say that three men (perhaps the Trinity, because they are referred to as "the LORD" several times) came calling on Abraham. Sarah fixed them a meal, and as they chatted, Sarah overheard them telling Abraham that God's promise to give them a child would soon be fulfilled.

Sarah, who had evidently given up hope, laughed. We don't know if it was a hearty chuckle or a quaint giggle, but the Lord heard it. In Genesis 18:13–14, He said: "Why did Sarah laugh? Does she doubt that she can have a child in her old age? I am the LORD! There is nothing too difficult for me. I'll come back next year at the time I promised, and Sarah will already have a son" (CEV).

Sarah denied laughing, but she was caught. (Why oh why do we try to argue with God? It's so fruitless!)

However, Sarah's disbelief turned into gratitude when she bore a son. Abraham and Sarah named the boy Isaac, which means "laughter." As she held her son, Sarah declared, "God has made me laugh. Now everyone will laugh with me" (Genesis 21:6 CEV).

This grateful woman had known plenty of scornful mirth; her society treated infertile women with ridicule and persecution. But now, she knew the best kind of laughter—the kind that comes from a heart buoyed by possibility and resurrected by hope.

I think Sarah also learned to laugh at herself. As a new mom at ninety-plus, don't you think she needed a great sense of humor just to get through each day? She had no MOPS group, no copy of *What to Expect the First Year*, nor disposable diapers. She lived in a tent, far from family and friends. And her husband was older than her—I'll bet he didn't get up in the night to help care for Isaac.

I'm sure she had to laugh, or she would have cried.

But you know, God wanted to give something much more

than a child to Sarah. He desired to change not just her life or her daily schedule, but her very soul. From an embarrassing encounter with the Lord, in which she hemmed and hawed and lied about laughing, to the birth of a baby named "Laughter," something happened to her. She got a hope transfusion. And when her son came in fulfillment of God's promise, she laughed, not cynically, but out of a full heart.

Comedian Anita Renfroe says, "Every woman has the chance to choose hilarity or insanity on a daily basis. Choose laughter."

Sarah chose laughter. Will we?

God wants to give us something more than what we're praying for. He wants to work in our lives so that joy bubbles up from our hearts, which He's filled to bursting with precious promises.

The question is: Will we let Him?

Allow Him to give you a hope transfusion. And when He does, act like a child. Giggle, dance, and sing. . .and give the glory back to Him.

GREAT THINGS ABOUT GETTING OLDER (COMPILED WITH HELP FROM FRIENDS):

1. Having time to travel. You're finally the big kid on the playground
2. For single women, not having to ask permission to do things or go somewhere
3. Less certainty, more willingness to embrace some of life's ambiguities
4. You're a mover and a shaker—just in different areas
5. For widows, discovering who you are on your own (with God)
6. Wisdom that comes from experience—and God's goodness
7. Seeing prayers answered
8. Finally owning a home or paying off a car
9. Selling your house and moving to a tiny apartment
10. Seeing your friends and family members come to know God
11. Little things don't bother you as much
12. Finally accepting yourself—and others—as God made you
13. Not caring so much what others think
14. Surprise parties
15. Trying new ice-cream flavors
16. Good memories
17. Deepening friendships
18. Simple joys are more meaningful

19. Liking fruits and veggies
20. For divorcees, a home life without constant conflict
21. Shopping for the kids and grandkids (less guilt)
22. Lunch with friends
23. Being friends with your parents (and your kids)
24. E-mail
25. DVDs
26. The Internet
27. Cell phones
28. Chick flicks with a gaggle of girlfriends
29. Staying up as late as you want (if you can stay awake)
30. Less fear about what others think
31. Experiencing Christmas through the eyes of a child
32. Being too old to be embarrassed by your folks
33. And too old to care if you embarrass your kids
34. If you forget something, you can blame it on your age
35. Great discounts at restaurants and other places
36. Looking through old yearbooks
37. *Antiques Roadshow*
38. Talk radio
39. Collecting great stories of God's faithfulness
40. Finding work you enjoy, and sticking with it
41. Everything old is new again (just wish you could fit into those pants from the '60s!)
42. More confidence in your abilities
43. Less stress about the things you can't do well
44. Faith that grows deeper
45. Hope that lasts longer

46. Love that grows stronger
47. Forgiveness that grows wider
48. Being here to enjoy it all
49. Realizing that being a child of God makes you ageless
50. And that with Him at our side, we don't have to fear getting older.

Also available

TURNING POINTS

Whose Kids *are* These?

REDISCOVERING LOVE AND
LAUGHTER AS A STEP-MOM
by Karon Phillips Goodman

The House is Quiet, *Now* What?

REDISCOVERING LIFE AND ADVENTURE AS
AN EMPTY NESTER
by Janice Hanna & Kathleen Y'Barbo

I Know I'm Not Alone, Lord

REDISCOVERING JOY
AND CONTENTMENT AFTER DIVORCE
by Janice Hanna & Kathleen Y'Barbo

Available wherever books are sold.